88 LIFE-CHANGING HIGH SCHOOL HACKS (A SUR-THRIVAL GUIDE™)

OPTIMIZE THE TEEN YEARS, UPGRADE YOUR LIFE SKILLS FAST, AND MASTER ADULTING BEFORE YOU GRADUATE

DEREK T FREEMAN

An imprint of DFT Virtual Ventures, LLC
Copyright © 2023 Derek T Freeman. All rights reserved.

The content within this book may not be reproduced, duplicated, or transmitted without direct written permission from the author or the publisher.

Under no circumstances will any blame or legal responsibility be held against the publisher, or author, for any damages, reparation, or monetary loss due to the information contained within this book, either directly or indirectly.

A Sur-Thrival Guide™ is a trademark of DFT Virtual Ventures, LLC

Legal Notice:

This book is copyright protected. It is only for personal use. You cannot amend, distribute, sell, use, quote, or paraphrase any part of this book's content without the author's or publisher's consent.

Disclaimer Notice:

Please note that the information contained within this document is for educational and entertainment purposes only. All effort has been expended to present accurate, up-to-date, reliable, and complete information. No warranties of any kind are declared or implied. Readers acknowledge that the author does not render legal, financial, medical, or professional advice. The content within this book has been derived from various sources. Please consult a licensed professional before attempting any techniques outlined in this book.

By reading this document, the reader agrees that under no circumstances is the author responsible for any direct or indirect losses incurred due to the use of the information contained within this document, including, but not limited to, errors, omissions, or inaccuracies.

ISBN: 979-8-9873806-2-8 (Paperback)
ISBN: 979-8-9873806-3-5 (Hardcover)

This book was written by a human and is dedicated to those who would take humanity to the next level. And my cats.

CONTENTS

Introduction — 13

1. SCHOOL & WORK ETHIC — 17
   Hack #1: Befriend Your Teachers — 18
   #2: Create Reward Systems — 20
   #3: Make a Whiteboard Out of Anything — 21
   #4: Use More Senses — 22
   #5: Do It Right the First Time/Don't Cut Corners — 23
   #6: filetype:pdf — 25
   #7: Fall in Love with Reading — 26
   #8: New School Rule — 28
   #9: Utilize Your (i)Phone — 29
   #10: Outsmart Burnout — 31
   #11: Ward off Pen Thieves — 33
   #12: Make It Micro — 33
   #13: Sleep on It (Part 1) — 35

2. TIME MANAGEMENT & PRODUCTIVITY — 37
   Hack #14: The Pomodoro Technique — 38
   #15: Move to the Music — 40
   #16: Prepare the Night Before — 41
   #17: The Eisenhower Matrix — 42
   #18: Eat the Frog — 45
   #19: Use a Calendar?? — 47
   #20: Mental Exaggeration — 49
   #21: Speed Reading — 51
   #22: Trigger Yourself to Sleep — 52
   #23: Block Distractions — 54
   #24: The Art of Not Multitasking — 57
   #25: The 80/20 Rule — 58

3. RELATIONSHIPS — 63
  Hack #26: Live from the Inside Out *(Self)* — 65
  #27: Befriend Your Parents *(Parents)* — 67
  #28: The Code Word *(Parents)* — 69
  #29: Pull the Awkward Convo Band-Aid off Quickly *(Parents)* — 70
  #30: The Code Phrase *(Parents/Friends)* — 72
  #31: "L.E.E.H.A." – The Five Qualities of a True Friend *(Friends)* — 73
  #32: The Art of Letting People Go *(Friends)* — 75
  #33: The Small Circle *(Friends)* — 77
  #34: Your Dating Barometer *(Dating)* — 80
  #35: Red-Flag Desperation *(Dating)* — 81
  #36: Don't Adult Yet *(Dating)* — 83
  #37: Ok, Now You Can Adult *(Dating)* — 84
  #38: Communicate C-l-e-a-r-l-y *(All)* — 87
  #39: Don't Use Them Wrong *(All)* — 88
  #40: Admit You're Wrong *(All)* — 89

4. HEALTH & HOME — 91
  Hack #41: Master the Microwave — 92
  #42: Five 5-Minute Recipes — 94
  #43: Prep for Success — 96
  #44: Linking Laundry — 98
  #45: Touch Ten — 99
  #46: The Toothbrush Revolution — 99
  #47: Befriend Your Vinegar — 101
  #48: Sell Your Stuff — 104
  #49: Mirror Magic — 105
  #50: The Big, Cool Water Bottle — 107
  #51: Simple Swaps — 109
  #52: Work in Weights — 111
  #53: Outsmart Overeating — 112

5. MONEY — 117
  Hack #54: View Money as Energy — 120
  #55: Master Basic Financial Literacy — 121
  #56: "Cash In" on Befriending Your Parents — 124

#57: Set Up Your Accounts ASAP	126
#58: Budget ASAP	127
#59: Don't Say I Never Gave You Anything	131
#60: Pay It Forward	133
#61: Forget About Debit	134
#62: Get It on Credit	135
#63: Seek Delayed Gratification (Part 1)	137
6. SPIRIT/ATTITUDE	**141**
Hack #64: Enjoy (In-Joy)	143
#65: The Path of Least Resistance	144
#66: Pay (with) Attention (Part 1)	148
#67: Believe In Belief	151
#68: Hold On Loosely	154
#69: Don't Battle Anything (The Seesaw of War)	157
#70: Be a Buffalo	160
#71: Sleep on It (Part 2)	162
#72: Know That You Know Nothing	164
#73: The Present (Read When Ready!)	167
7. JOB & CAREER	**175**
Hack #74: Go Your Own Way	177
#75: Diversify Now, Streamline Later	181
#76: Respond to AI with HI (Not What You Think!)	182
#77: Nail Any Interview	184
#78: The Art of Letting People In	186
#79: Don't Be Best, Be Unrivaled	188
#80: Seek Delayed Gratification (Part 2)	190
#81: The Ultimate Success Secret	192
8. BONUS - CARS!	**195**
Hack #82: Humility First	197
#83: Master Basic Maintenance	198
#84: Pay (with) Attention (Part 2)	199
#85: ¼ Is the New "E"	201
#86: Equip for Emergencies	201

#87: The Dos and Don'ts of Tailgating	203
#88: See and Be Seen	205
Conclusion	209
References	211
About the Author	217

JOIN MY MAILING LIST FOR A CHANCE TO GET MY NEXT BOOK FOR FREE!

***NO SPAM

FOLLOW MY SOCIALS

INTRODUCTION

hack (hak)

verb

1. to cough roughly or harshly.

*"The patient with emphysema is **hacking** all day."*

Oops, wait a minute…

Ok – here we go:

hack (hak)

noun

1. a good solution or piece of advice; a strategy or technique for managing one's time or activities more efficiently.

Much better! The goal of this book is straightforward (and it's not about coughing). It's to help you manage your adolescent years more effectively so that you don't just survive but **thrive** as an adult. In other words, we'll be "hacking" or "efficiently managing" the high school experience for the **benefit of the future**.

I use the term "high school" loosely. For much of the following advice, "where" or "how" you do your schooling shouldn't really matter. What matters is being able to enter adulthood easily and on your terms. What matters is *owning your life instead of IT owning YOU*.

That, in my opinion, is "adulting." For what it's worth, I'm 41 years old at the time of writing this, yet I have the heart of an 18-year-old. Adulting shouldn't make you lose your spark, curiosity, or sense of adventure. It shouldn't make you boring - or bored. Growing up can be tricky - it can turn us into a shell of what we once loved about ourselves if we let it.

This book aims to bridge the gap between "young adult" and "adult." An alternate title (although less catchy) might be "Start Mastering Your Life Early On." I believe teens are capable of MUCH more than they're often given credit for. Curriculums teach many of the "hows," but what about the "whys"? *The whys are where the power lies.* Therefore, you're about to read some things you will not be taught in school! It would be my honor to help you grab life by the horns, and I'd love to help you learn how to do that in easy, manageable ways - before the stresses pile up and things become more difficult to change.

Speaking of the title - **don't be misled by it**. This is not a collection of recycled, worn-out cliches. No, this is a compilation of work that was deeply researched and profoundly inspired (it does get pretty deep). It's a resource you can read linearly or bounce around with as sections become relevant to your life.

You may notice a few things as you read:

1) There's a wide range of hacks. You'll discover some game-changing advice that I *personally* swear by and some fun little tricks that are easy to implement. There is also everything in between, in one big melting pot. This passion project was written whimsically - I had a lot of fun with it! And if some hacks seem a little more evident than others, know they're in here for a reason.

2) There is no "fat" in this book. In other words, you won't have to do much digging to get to the gold. Although there are stories, they are only meant to drive home points and allow you to internalize the techniques. A *ton* of helpful information is coming your way, so don't feel pressured to remember it all – that's why it's written down!

3) Finally, each hack is numbered, making it super simple to jot down the ones you might want to revisit – because some might resonate with you right now, while others may align better down the road.

And now for our feature presentation!

I hope you benefit from each nugget of wisdom for many years to come.

1

SCHOOL & WORK ETHIC

"The pessimist complains about the wind; the optimist expects it to change; the realist adjusts the sails."

— WILLIAM ARTHUR WARD

I like this quote because it shows how easy it can be to achieve better results.

For decades and decades, it's been imprinted on us that to be successful in school or work, we need to put in long hours and break our backs. "Nothing is ever accomplished without hard work!" If you're not burnt out and exhausted by the end of the day, you didn't do enough - right?

Well, no. I don't mean to downplay "hard work." I just never thought it was worded correctly. The truth is, there are much more innovative and efficient ways to achieve great results without having to sacrifice so much of our time and energy.

"Work smarter, not harder." Now that's a quote I like. There are dozens of ways to become more productive, find better focus, and thrive in school - whether it be public, private, home, or in some cases, unschooling. Again - I use "high school" as a general term for the age range this information is geared towards. But really, a refined work ethic will carry you much farther.

Your goal should be to develop the ability to **take control of your learning and working environment**. To "set the sail" and let the wind work *for* you, whenever possible...

HACK #1: BEFRIEND YOUR TEACHERS

What it's not: Just another way of getting your teachers to give you higher marks. Pretending to be their best friend. Trying to bribe them. Sucking up.

What it is: A chance to engage with and create a relationship with a significant character in your life that extends beyond the classroom walls.

Good relationships with your teachers can help you stay motivated and give you great insight into the subject matter.

Furthermore, developing solid friendships can sometimes last a lifetime! It's about *forming connections* with your teachers and seeing them as educators and mentors.

How can you do this?

1) Feel free to seek assistance when you need it.

2) Visit them during office hours or extra credit periods.

3) Hold more meaningful conversations.

4) Express your appreciation when they go above and beyond to help you succeed.

5) Go so far as to send a thank you note at the end of the term or semester.

(When homeschooling, your parent may double as your teacher. Similar strategies may still be applied, but we'll expand on that later.)

Being a respectful and enthusiastic student will generally benefit you *everywhere*. You never know when you'll need a little extra "cushion," like a deadline extension or an extra day to complete a test. The more you prove your commitment, the more the benefits will show. A teacher or mentor who sees you are invested is more likely to invest in **you**.

#2: CREATE REWARD SYSTEMS

I believe goals are essential, but I don't think they're powerful enough on their own. Employing strategies to motivate yourself will **supercharge** your effectiveness. That's why I suggest the establishment of reward systems. And by creating your *own* reward systems (rather than having your parents or teachers set them for you), you will empower yourself and kickstart self-accountability.

Rewards don't have to be extravagant or over-the-top. They can be as simple as ice cream or a night out - anything that will encourage you and make working toward the goal more enjoyable. However, if your rewards are substantial enough, you will be *more* likely to stay on track and finish your tasks.

I used to make a deal with myself that after every 45 minutes of studying, I get 15 minutes of "free" time (like watching TV, grabbing a snack, or playing video games). I still more or less use that strategy to avoid burnout!

Here are some more basic examples:

- Eating your favorite food if you complete work early
- Spending time outside the house only after finishing a specific assignment
- A movie night after a week of staying on track
- Going out with friends only once chores are completed

- Buying a new item of clothing for every "A" on your report card
- A day off from studying when you knock out a long-term project

Only YOU know your specific goals and what it takes to motivate yourself. Strategically set up rewards to leverage areas where you need an extra "push."

I suggest writing these down in a dedicated notebook or something you can hang on your wall. (**Mini-hack:** Writing is such a powerful tool - it helps "cement" the rewards or goals into your subconscious. Writing something down helps retain information *way* more than reading or typing.)

Further, inform someone who can also hold you accountable, like a parent or close friend, about your reward system. Raise the stakes and make it "real" by involving someone else. Who knows, your parents might even feel inspired to jump in on the deal!

#3: MAKE A WHITEBOARD OUT OF ANYTHING

Your entire life might implode without to-do lists if you're anything like me. And what's one of the best ways to keep a list? A whiteboard!

But what if you don't have a whiteboard or enough wall space for one? Don't worry - I got your back. A "whiteboard" can be made out of almost anything:

- Mirrors
- Plastic plates
- Vinyl
- Metal (unpainted)
- Frames
- Glass
- Shower curtains
- A chalkboard or flat surface with chalkboard paint
- A DVD or video game case(!)

Keep a pack of *dry-erase markers* handy - then you can wipe your notes clean with an eraser, cloth, or damp paper towel.

Obviously, you could keep notes on your phone. But for those of us who are more visceral, spontaneously writing and drawing on things is a cool way to get ideas out and truly express them (remember what I said about the power of writing).

#4: USE MORE SENSES

Usually, when you finish a paper, essay, or assignment, you glance it over once or twice, then turn it in - right?

I bet you never realized that during this process, you only used **two** of the five senses - *sight* and *touch*.

Well, have you ever tried *listening* to what you wrote? You'd be shocked at how differently it comes across. Try copying and pasting your project into a translator (Google,

Microsoft, iTranslate, Speechify, etc.), and let it read the words back to you. Listening to your work can help you catch mistakes and typos, but it will also show you how it *feels*.

I'm not done yet. Now, SPEAK your work out loud. How does it flow? How does it make you feel? Does it project convincingly? Does it force you to notice spots that need minor adjustments? By utilizing your other senses, I guarantee you will bump up your quality of work by at **least** 15% - and it's quicker than you think (I haven't figured out how to incorporate smell yet).

Guess what? I'm using this technique right now. Does this hack-ception blow your mind? It will once you start doing it.

#5: DO IT RIGHT THE FIRST TIME/DON'T CUT CORNERS

If you apply it, this one will be an invaluable cornerstone of your work ethic. Let me tell you a little story.

I was 16 when I got my first job ever. It wasn't anything fancy. A family friend owned a cleaning business, and because of that connection, I had dibs on the job.

At basically minimum wage, a few of us would sweep, mop, and wax supermarket floors two or three nights a week. It was pretty labor-intensive. On the big jobs, we would pull all-nighters. But it was my first experience of earning my own money - and that was awesome.

Generally, we would sweep the entire floor first (often they were large stores, like Walmarts), then go over and give them a good mop, and then coats of wax when needed.

Occasionally, the boss would lock us in with a supervisor while he went to take care of other business. My co-workers and I thought we were smart: "Do we really need to sweep this *entire* floor? Let's just hit the rough spots and get it over with." So, we would do a "skim" with the broom, fool around for a while, and then mop.

You can probably see where this is going.

Turns out, sweeping is the first step for a reason in this whole cleaning thing. When we started to mop, all the dust, dirt, and debris which we initially ignored started to gum together and build up. Not only did it ruin the mop water, but the floors actually started to look *worse*! The kicker was that after our boss returned and looked everything over, he told us to start again with the brooms because the wax would seal the gunk into the floor. Oops.

The moral here is that 1) incorrectly performing the first step resulted in a worse outcome, and 2) trying to cut corners *doubled* our labor because we had to redo it all!

This tale is only a basic example of my point, but there's a reason it stuck with me all these years: it can be applied to almost **everything**.

Writing a paper? Do proper research first. Create a killer outline.

Making home improvements? Avoid trying to get away with using cheap materials - it will ironically result in money loss, frustration, and time wasted.

Regarding any project, putting some care into each step will make your life *way* easier in the long run. Plus, you'll be well-respected and stand out from all the hacks (pun intended).

Do it right the first time. Don't cut corners - the benefits are an illusion. There is a reason for order! And only mop after sweeping.

#6: FILETYPE:PDF

If you've misplaced or forgotten a textbook, you can usually find it in PDF format on Google. Sometimes, this could save you money as you might avoid buying new books every semester.

Including "filetype:pdf" in your Google searches can instantly pull up full books. It restricts the results to PDF files, so no more searching through unnecessary websites or obsolete material - just the good stuff. This prompt is a handy tool when researching pretty much *anything* online. Simply type "filetype:pdf" after your search query.

For instance, if you were researching a paper on renewable energy sources, you could search for "renewable energy sources filetype:pdf," which would then show strictly PDF documents regarding renewable energy. Give it a try! It's a time-saver and a very cool trick in general.

#7: FALL IN LOVE WITH READING

This is not so much a "hack" as it is an eye-opener encouraging you to take advantage of something you may not already be.

At the time of writing this, my children are just barely approaching their teens. And you know what? I can't even get them to commit to reading my first book! I think it would be a tragedy if reading books became nothing more than a "chore."

Knowledge is one of the most powerful tools in your arsenal. Extensive reading can put you ahead in any school or work setting. But OH - it's so much more than that. Check out these very real "side effects" that come along with reading:

1) Increased Vocabulary. Reading will not only help you understand words and their meanings better, but it will also expose you to variations of the *same* word. This will improve your writing and communication skills, making them more robust and efficient. Additionally, as you use language more effectively, you'll be able to understand both yourself and those around you better.

2) Improved Memory. As you read, your brain must retrieve and store information from the text so that it continues to make sense. Over time, this "training" can assist in boosting your overall memory and focus.

3) Enhanced Imagination. Reading tends to create vivid mental images and scenarios, intensifying your imagination and creativity. This is especially important when composing stories or devising creative solutions to problems.

4) Heightened Analytical Thinking. Books encourage critical thinking by exposing readers to many points of view and character motivations. This can help us better grasp the world and make better life decisions!

5) Stress Relief. According to studies, reading can lower stress levels by as much as 68%. Given life's hecticness, this is a great method for decompressing and unwinding. Getting lost in a book can provide a temporary escape to a different world, taking your mind off worries and negative thoughts.

Don't read just because you have to. Read because you want to learn and explore. Read to supercharge your power! Numerous books are available on any topic you could possibly be interested in. Choose the ones that pique your interest and start reaping the benefits.

#8: NEW SCHOOL RULE

Transitioning to a new school - or even trickier, a new school *system* - can be **very** overwhelming (check out my previous book, "Building Unstoppable Self-Confidence for Teens," for my own story).

By being familiar with your destination ahead of time, however, you can alleviate a great deal of anxiety and tension. This way, you will already have an understanding of what to anticipate so that you can avoid any additional stress.

Create a rule that you must **visit a new school in advance** (more than once, if necessary) to learn the lay of the land. This will automatically give you an edge in two regards: 1) attitude and mindset (you're going to make the most of this new opportunity and take control!), and 2) familiarization with the school physically beforehand (a vital step to help ease the transition).

Here's how:

- Take a tour of the new building (via an open house or orientation) to get a feel for where things are located (classrooms, cafeteria, library, bathrooms, etc.).
- Get to know the school administration and other faculty (such as your teachers) so that you feel more familiar on the first day.

- Ask an upper-level student you may know (a sibling, family friend, or neighbor) to give you a more personalized tour of the building and provide insight into what it's like to be a student there.
- Understand the school's rules - what is and isn't allowed?
- Network with other students right off the bat so you feel like you can hit the ground running as soon as the year starts.

This technique will give you an instant advantage to start on the right foot. It works for middle school, high school, college, and also jobs!

#9: UTILIZE YOUR (I)PHONE

A) I constantly use my iPhone as a **calculator**. In fact, it's the *only* calculator I use. But what always drove me crazy was the inability (or so I thought) to delete ONE digit instead of clearing the whole screen and starting over. When I came across this hack in my research, I learned: that you *CAN*. Just swipe left or right on the numbers at the top part of the screen. It's that easy!

B) The **calculator** app also has a hidden trick that makes it even more helpful. By flipping the phone to sideways orientation, you can switch to a scientific calculator. This is perfect for higher-level math studies, such as Algebra and

Calculus. And remember, you can have Siri input the numbers for you, too.

C) Your **lock screen** can be a *very* efficient, quick way to access information on the go. Use your lock screen to display your schedule, notes, or even a motivational quote. Only you will know what's necessary. You can map out the most pertinent details of your agenda on a single page – just use your imagination. (*Side note: I wouldn't put anything too private there that you wouldn't want others to see.*)

D) Try setting **alarms** for upcoming classes and tests so you never miss an important event. Utilize **reminders** to help keep track of homework and other tasks, and set yourself up with **calendar notifications** before due dates and special events arrive.

E) You can use the "**Voice Memos**" app to record classes or meetings you'd like to revisit and share with friends who need them. This will allow you instant access to any detail you might've missed. Once the voice memo is complete, save it and tap the "export" button to share it via iMessage or email. Play it back at a higher speed to find critical points quicker. Just make sure 1) you're allowed to do it, and 2) you set your phone to "do not disturb" or "airplane mode"!

These tips would've saved me lots of frustration in the past. It makes me wonder what other iPhone hacks I don't know about.

#10: OUTSMART BURNOUT

Burnout is all too common among high school students. Why? Because it's easy to get caught up in the hectic schedule and expectations of getting good grades, "achieving excellence," and "being successful." The pressure to perform flawlessly and be "the best" can overwhelm young people while they juggle social lives, sports, after-school activities, and other commitments. Almost inevitably, this results in an unsustainable amount of stress.

As the workload intensifies during the school year (junior and senior years especially), so do the chances of burnout. It'll make you feel bad about yourself, leading to erratic decision-making, fatigue, and lack of motivation. The last thing you want is to push yourself so hard that you reach your breaking point - it's never worth it.

> *"Burnout is the result of too much energy output and not enough energy self-invested. In other words, it's burning more fuel than you've put in your tank."*
>
> — MELISSA STEGINUS

The truth is that you don't have to go until you crash. Instead of allowing "work" to define your adolescent years, you can employ small, simple strategies to stay motivated and productive without succumbing to burnout. The following are the most effective methods I've discovered:

1) You need YOU time. Plain and simple. You're not a robot, and your parents or guardians shouldn't expect you to be. These years are a balancing act, for sure. But I promise that if you maintain a level head and stay focused when needed, you can approach your parents explaining how you'll be "blocking out certain hours of the day and week for self-care." I guarantee you their jaws will drop (in a good way).

2) Just say "no" (why does that sound familiar?). Don't take on more than you can handle; don't feel obligated to go above and beyond to impress others. What does it matter if someone else can juggle more than you can? That's their life, not yours. If it were up to everyone else, we'd all be run ragged. *You know what you are capable of.* This mentality doesn't imply cutting yourself short and underachieving. It's about learning to say "no" when you genuinely feel stretched too thin.

3) Get help when you need it. It's never wrong to seek assistance; I would encourage it. Don't be afraid to reach out and put yourself in a better position. Whether it's a tutor, teacher, academic advisor, coach, parent, or even a friend - the goal is to *avoid falling so far behind that you can't catch up.* Even if your grades start to slip, there's still time to correct the situation. Take this step **before** you become overwhelmed!

#11: WARD OFF PEN THIEVES

Remember, I'm including *all* sorts of hacks, from big to small.

Well, this might be the smallest. And it is, admittedly, so trivial that I almost left it out. But you know what? I don't care - it's too funny and practical not to include!

We all know how people *love* stealing pens and how frustrating it is *not* to have one when you need it. Little less known is that **red** pens rarely get stolen - because, well, they're red.

So, buy a bunch of red pens and *switch out the refills* with some high-quality black or blue ink. Voila - no one is tempted to take your good pens anymore!

#12: MAKE IT MICRO

A few years ago, I was working on the cover art for one of my band's albums. A good friend of mine, who is incredibly talented in visual art, came up with multiple designs and options for me to choose from. It quickly got overwhelming, getting lost in all the nuance, detail, and endless decision-making. I was like, "These are ALL so good - it's going to be impossible to choose!"

Then he showed me a trick I will utilize forever. "Ok, let's try making them smaller," he said. "Then we'll know which images are the best." A little confused, I went with it.

We shrunk all the images down. We would even go into other rooms and look at them from a distance to gain a different perspective. We compared them to other album covers at the same scale. Almost instantly, the best options popped right out. It became much easier to tell what worked and what didn't because we started looking at the **essence** of the art rather than the details that *make up* the essence.

Think about when you're shopping for a book, poster, or music on your phone. At these proportions, our eyes can ironically see the "big picture." That's why intelligent visual artists create designs that stand out, catch your attention, and deliver the story even when *tiny*.

You can apply this knowledge to any art or visual project you may be working on. If you find yourself losing perspective, take a picture of the project. Come back to it later and look at it small; even put it side by side with something comparable.

Need help deciding if an outfit works? Lay out your clothes and take a pic of a few different options. Look at them compared to each other as thumbnails - you will know which outfits work and which don't.

The real-life, even bigger picture here (hah!) is that when we zoom too closely into *anything*, we lose perspective on what the thing really **is**. In essence, **we need to focus on what matters**. Sit with that one for a while! How many ways can you apply this to your own life experience?

#13: SLEEP ON IT (PART 1)

Do you ever wonder how your heart, lungs, and organs operate *perfectly* while sleeping? How about how your hair and nails grow and your food continues to digest? These phenomena are possible because your **subconscious mind** runs your vital functions.

The subconscious mind is extraordinarily potent. It's the part of you that works without you having to "consciously" think about it, and it controls so much more than you could ever imagine. Also, the subconscious *never stops*.

That's right - this mysterious part of us (which makes up about 95% of our brainpower and is millions of times faster than the conscious mind) can solve problems, retain information, and drive creativity *while we sleep.*

Although you may have yet to understand it fully, the practice of #13 is simple: dwell on the things you want to learn and remember **as you fall asleep** - whether it's a history timeline, a scientific equation, French vocabulary terms, prepping for a test, or simply recalling facts and ideas. I'm telling you - this is an art! Learn to meditate on your desires as you drift off in bed. Your subconscious will then take control and analyze the information, with you seemingly unaware.

The next day, you will be amazed at how much easier it is to comprehend and remember the material. Not only will it feel like you understand the concepts better, but your memory retention skills may also improve.

Why? Because no conscious ideas interfere with your subconscious mind while you sleep. It can accomplish whatever you "suggest to it" without being distracted. And, given that we spend around one-third of our lives sleeping, that is a *lot* of valuable time to take advantage of.

Keep this practice up - eventually, you'll be able to tap into the infinite, immense powers of the subconscious mind in many other ways.

2

TIME MANAGEMENT & PRODUCTIVITY

" Give me six hours to chop down a tree and I will spend the first four sharpening the axe."

— ABRAHAM LINCOLN

Make no mistake – if you can learn to manage your time wisely at a young age, even a little bit, you are far ahead of the pack.

Life moves quickly during high school, and it's easy (even natural) to become overwhelmed by the enormous amount of work that needs to be done. Regardless, you ought to be making the most of your youth - so isn't it a no-brainer to use your time more efficiently?

Not using effective time management techniques is like choosing a typewriter over a MacBook. With the right techniques, you can increase your personal time *while* maximizing your potential, streamlining your daily tasks, and increasing your productivity.

This section will teach you how to do just that - manage your time and organize your day better. We'll also talk about how to deal with distractions and stay laser-focused on the things that matter. You'll learn why it's critical to set goals and then break them down into tasks you can complete in manageable chunks. Finally, you'll learn how to increase your energy levels to make the most of every day.

HACK #14: THE POMODORO TECHNIQUE

I'd heard of this time-flow technique for quite some time, yet I never knew till now what a "Pomodoro" was. Spoiler alert: it's a tomato.

Francesco Cirillo, an Italian software developer and student who wanted to increase productivity, created the Pomodoro Technique in the late 1980s. The technique is about breaking down large tasks into small, manageable portions of time.

Here's the concept: choose your goal or task and set a timer for **25 minutes**. *Don't let anything distract you from focusing on that task for 25 minutes.* After the timer goes off, take a **five-minute** break to refresh your mind. That half hour equals one "Pomodoro." Start another 25 minutes of intense focus after that.

You can go even longer by combining four Pomodoros, then rewarding yourself with a longer 15 to 30-minute break. This helps you to stay motivated and avoid losing steam in the long run.

It would look something like this:

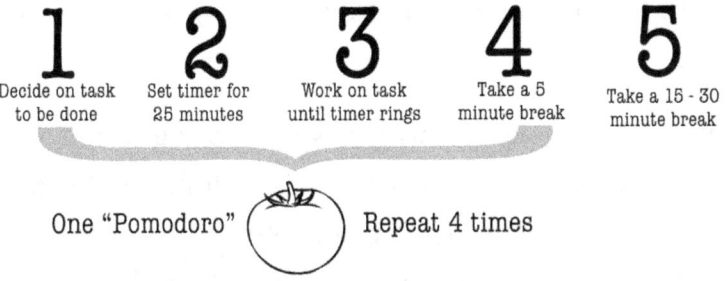

What makes it work?

Breaking up the workload into smaller chunks can help you retain more information. It reduces distractions by limiting the work window, making it easier to focus on one thing at a time without becoming overwhelmed. It will help you overcome procrastination by encouraging *small steps forward*. Finally, the frequent breaks will replenish energy levels for focusing on more tasks ahead. These reasons make the

Pomodoro Technique (and even customized versions) an awesome way to **hack** studying.

Are you thinking, "Why a tomato?" The technique was named after the *tomato-shaped kitchen timer* once popular in Italy – the one Francesco used when creating it!

#15: MOVE TO THE MUSIC

There's a little trick I used to use in the mornings when getting ready for school. I always thought it was *my* trick, but now I'm beginning to find it's actually a *thing*. Let me explain.

Throughout my youth, music was everything to me. I would get very obsessed with certain bands, albums, and songs and often listen to them on repeat. When my favorite band Silverchair released their second album, I would play the CD every morning as soon as I got up. Eventually, I noticed that the time it took me to get ready for school was equivalent to the *first five tracks on the album*. It was a timer! But good news - you don't have to have a CD player for this trick (I would never ask such a thing of you).

Make a custom playlist of songs that *equals the time it takes you to get ready for school*. Pretty soon, your morning schedule will work according to specific songs, and you will automatically know when you're running late, early, or right on time.

You don't have to limit this to the morning, either! You can make a playlist for ANY routine period you may have and adjust the style of music to fit the theme. It's a great way to subliminally hint your **timing** back at you without constantly having to check the **time**.

#16: PREPARE THE NIGHT BEFORE

Let's continue the theme of getting ready for school with this little prequel. It's targeted at those of you who, like me, find the action part of "rise and shine" quite burdensome.

Preparing the night before might sound like common sense, but let me ask: "Do *you* do it?" If not, consider the benefits: 1) you'll be able to wake up later, possibly creating more sleep time for yourself, and 2) you won't have to think nearly as much about specifics in the morning (I find it hard to think about *anything* in that groggy state after waking up).

I'll make it as easy as possible for you and give some ideas:

- Shower at night. You may even sleep better (definitely cleaner).
- Pack your bag with all the supplies you need for tomorrow - the right books, materials, etc.
- Set out your clothes for the next day - including shoes and socks.

- If you're bringing lunch, pre-make it and store it in the fridge so all you have to do in the morning is grab it.
- Plan a leisurely breakfast: cereal, toast, yogurt, fruit, cheese & crackers - whatever works for you. Prepare what you can, but if anything, simply deciding beforehand will save time.
- Set your alarm and put it somewhere across the room, forcing you to get out of bed in the morning. Either way, you have to do it - might as well pull that band-aid off quickly.
- Make your alarm tone pleasant and energizing instead of a familiar sound that triggers the horrors of waking.

You get the point. If you're not a morning person, *make it easier on yourself*. Utilize the previous night and set yourself up to glide through the AM effortlessly.

#17: THE EISENHOWER MATRIX

What it's not: Just a really, really cool name.

What it is: An easy-to-use tool that can help you become more focused and efficient with your time.

	URGENT	**NOT URGENT**
IMPORTANT	Quadrant I *urgent and important* **DO**	Quadrant II *not urgent but important* **PLAN**
NOT IMPORTANT	Quadrant III *urgent but not important* **DELEGATE**	Quadrant IV *not urgent and not important* **ELIMINATE**

Take your to-do list for the day or week and divide it up into four quadrants:

1) Urgent and Important: These tasks need to be done - and soon.

2) Not Urgent but Important: Tasks that may not have hard deadlines but still need to be planned.

3) Urgent but Not Important: Tasks that should be done soon but could be delegated or outsourced (meaning a friend or family member could do it).

4) Not Urgent and Not Important: These aren't at the top of the list - they don't have to be done immediately, and sometimes not at all.

Once done, your matrix may look something like this (although cleaning your room might be more of a priority for you):

	Urgent!	Not Urgent
Important	Finish history project Doctor appt.	Workout Finish book Call Jeff back
Not Important	Get concert tix Clean cat box	Wash the car Clean room Beat game

The Eisenhower Matrix (or "Box") will help you focus on important responsibilities instead of wasting time on "low-value" and unimportant ones, which many of us do. It can assist you in making decisions, quickly identifying the things that require your attention, and taking control of your time management. It's a very straightforward yet effective way to prioritize your to-do lists.

Bonus: There are plenty of apps that do this, too. Search "Eisenhower Matrix" in the app store, and a bunch will pop up. Find the one that works best for you. That way, you don't have to...you know, draw stuff like I did.

#18: EAT THE FROG

Did you know frogs are an excellent source of energy? You may even find them quite tasty, depending on how you cook them.

Although that might be true, you probably don't want to bring frogs to school for lunch. And that's also not what #18 is about.

The expression "eat the frog" refers to a productivity technique proposed by Mark Twain in which you begin your day by tackling the thing you *least want to do* (the "frog"). It's about getting the most challenging, unappealing task over with right away - allowing everything after that to glide effortlessly. As a rule of thumb - eat the biggest frog first!

> *"Eat a live frog first thing in the morning and nothing worse will happen to you the rest of the day."*
>
> — MARK TWAIN

The benefit of this strategy is that it **crushes** procrastination immediately. Procrastination is a pure time-waster, but we all do it (author included). Heck, I've even procrastinated over writing sections about procrastination!

You should easily be able to identify your "big frogs" - they reside in the pit of your stomach and feel very **significant**. You'll encounter resistance to them and feel pressure to avoid them. Frogs include things like organization, project planning, meetings, awkward conversations with people, and other things you don't want to do because they *aren't fun*.

It's always tempting to put the hardest things off till later. However, if you can overcome your resistance and complete them first thing in the day, you'll be surprised at how much more productive you'll be for the *rest* of the day - and how much better you'll feel. In my opinion, that feeling of relief early on is worth its weight in gold.

Bonus: *The Five Best Frog Recipes for Teens!*

Eh, next book, maybe.

#19: USE A CALENDAR??

OK, OK - I can read your mind right now. "This book is supposed to be giving me life-changing secrets! Calendars are like, ancient...is he really telling me that using a calendar will change my life??" And I would respond with - YES.

YES, I AM.

The humble calendar is one of the greatest (and easiest) tools you can use to be more effective. It's an essential element for keeping track of your life. It will allow you to plan ahead, visualize what's coming up, and, most importantly - free your mind.

The calendar is hidden right beneath your nose, and I bet you don't use it. I've noticed plenty of adults use calendars (that's why they're still around and like, ancient), but rarely do young people. You may not feel the need, but remember - we're setting you up to **master adulting.** At first, it may feel like a chore or an extra job - but here's the ironic part: for the few seconds or so it takes to put something on the calendar (it can be fun stuff, too), you are creating massive freedom and space in your mind and your life. You *might* even become addicted to this.

For myself, I like a traditional calendar. It hangs in the kitchen where I can constantly be aware of what the weeks ahead hold for me. Plus, I made it on Vistaprint, and the theme is my CATS. Nevertheless, you can also use a digital calendar on your phone and fit a lot more info that way.

Start putting things on your calendar - chores, study times, dates with friends, or special events you can't miss. It's YOUR space - honestly, just be creative and put whatever you want there! You won't have to remember as much. You'll disappoint others less. Your life will flow much, much smoother.

Bonus: You'll *need* a calendar when you're a full-fledged adult. By making it part of your routine now, it'll feel completely natural once it comes time for the big stuff.

#20: MENTAL EXAGGERATION

The following two hacks are indeed latent superpowers.

This one involves memory retention. First, you should know that our brains process 90% of information **visually**. Additionally, we process pictures 60,000 times quicker than words (Wong 2021). We can already use this knowledge to improve our memory. But there's more...

Our brains also crave **novelty** (or uniqueness) and react more strongly to *bizarre* things. Novelty triggers dopamine (a "reward" chemical in the brain that makes us feel good) and encourages us to **remember** the experience (Lazer 2020). You can use this to your advantage by exaggerating a scenario to stand out in your mind (don't worry, this will all come together).

With mental exaggeration, you take an image in your mind and make it absurdly HUGE, *intense*, or oUtRaGeOuS. Use as much color and detail as you can. The more extreme it is, the better your recall will be.

So, how can you use this to help you remember things? Here are a few examples:

- If you need to remember a shopping list, visualize an elephant picking up each item from the shelves and placing it in its trunk as it walks through the grocery store.
- If you need to remember someone's name, imagine the person covered in glitter or wearing a costume with their name written all over it.
- If you need to remember an address, picture a giant castle with the street number in big, bold letters.

Although mental exaggeration is great for remembering, it's also a great trick when you need an extra burst of motivation. It's simple: imagine your future self in the best possible scenario, then exaggerate it tenfold. For instance, if you need to finish a tedious project, picture yourself crossing the finish line in an Olympic race and imagine how amazing that feeling would be. Maybe tons of talking animals crowd around you, congratulating you on completing that specific thing. I know it's odd, but this can fuel your momentum and push you to get started or keep going.

#21: SPEED READING

You will never escape reading for the rest of your life (not that you should want to). Books, magazines, online articles, text messages, emails, notes, reports - you'll forever be reading something daily.

I used to have this problem of reading a paragraph and then completely forgetting what I read, forcing me to go back and reread it. Well, not anymore. This EASY trick allows you to **read faster** and **increase focus** simultaneously.

It's as simple as guiding your eyes across each line of text with a "visual pacer" (like a pen or finger). Because your eyes are drawn to movement, this creates a sort of "invisible speed limit" for you, keeping you on track and ensuring you don't lose focus. However, this is only half of the hack.

You'll want to do this with your **left hand** (or your right hand if you are naturally left-handed). This is because *the right side of your brain controls the left side of your body*. And since the right brain is in charge of creativity and problem-solving, using the visual pacer with your left hand will allow you to speed up your reading without losing comprehension or focus. The right brain's creativity will even trigger your other senses more powerfully, allowing you to recall information more readily and experience the words viscerally (Kotler 2013)!

This all happens automatically in your subconscious - it is an incredible technique. Try reading this very colorful paragraph using your left pointer finger as a pacer:

"The sky was a stunning electric blue, stretching far and wide. The birds joyously chirped overhead, and the light warmed my skin. I took a deep breath and felt the fresh air fill my lungs. Inhaling, I tasted salt in the breeze. Exhaling, I was overcome with gratitude for a beautiful July day. As I watched fluffy clouds glide by, I felt a serene sensation that could not be matched."

I have been transported to the beach. Thanks, right brain!

#22: TRIGGER YOURSELF TO SLEEP

I won't lie to you - I'm a night owl. I can't help it. I love staying up late and sleeping in, and I always have. However, the harsh reality is that sleep deprivation can severely impair your health, life, and happiness. It is vital, *especially* for teenagers, to get enough sleep to be alert and perform well during the day (school or not).

There are many ways to improve your sleep routine: avoiding caffeine late in the day, putting screens away at least an hour before bed, keeping a regular sleep pattern, etc. But if you're still having trouble sleeping, it may be due to a lack of an evening "shutdown" routine.

A proper shutdown routine consists of sleep "triggers." This is the most reliable method I've personally used. It works like this: you identify a specific activity or object with rest, and the more frequently you perform it, the more your brain will recognize it as an invitation to...pass the **** out.

If falling asleep is a problem, consider creating a night-time ritual. Some ideas:

- Take a hot shower before bed
- Read a book (Derek T Freeman is a suggested author)
- Light some candles
- Focus on breathwork (slow, deep breathing)
- Burn essential oils such as lavender
- Drink hot tea
- Play calming music or nature sounds

...or any combination of preferred activities. Eventually, you'll create a beautiful bedtime ritual that signals your brain: "Night-night!"

To make this work, you must keep the routine consistent - try to do it at the same time each night, and don't skip or break the habit too frequently. The goal is to **create a mental link between your ritual and sleeping**. You'll soon be able to fall asleep almost instantly (it will even work any time during the day).

Alright, that's enough. All the sleep talk is putting me to sleep.

#23: BLOCK DISTRACTIONS

The easy part about helping you block distractions is providing you with the methods. The tricky (but most important) part is conveying *why* it's necessary so you feel compelled to do it!

Distractions can be a formidable foe if not carefully managed and controlled. A distraction is anything that *diverts your attention from what you're focusing on*, reducing your productivity. Believe it or not, most distractions come from within rather than from without. You must be aware of the **thoughts and feelings leading to procrastination** to block out distractions effectively.

Again, I speak from experience. Distractions can be a big problem for me. If I don't have a plan, my focus tends to waver - then I waste valuable time and annoy myself.

If you're like me and find yourself unable to concentrate or easily distracted, you'll need a take-charge approach. Begin by identifying the *sources* of your distractions. What are the things that usually keep you from focusing? Pay attention to which ones trigger you as you read these common examples:

- social media
- phone notifications
- noise in your environment
- people talking to you
- television

- video games
- internet browsing
- music
- pets

These can also be distractions:

- worry and fear
- daydreaming
- boredom/restlessness
- overthinking

Once you've targeted the little buggers (aka sources of distraction), you can begin to block them out. Here are the methods:

1) **The "no-distraction zone."** Create a place to FOCUS, whether it's your bedroom, a corner of your house, or a place you frequent (like a cafe). Remember the idea of triggering yourself to sleep by creating a mental link? Your new zone should do the same - only this time, it should trigger **productivity**.

2) **Turn off all notifications.** Nothing is more distracting than your phone buzzing or something popping up on your laptop every few seconds. To take this further, consider airplane mode or even putting your phone in another room (zipping it up in your bag if you're not home).

3) Get organized. A cluttered physical environment often leads to a cluttered mind. Before you begin working, clear your workspace and organize everything you need. Know where your materials are so you don't waste time looking for them later.

4)" Do Not Disturb" hours. Be clear about the times you won't be available and stick to them. If your family and friends will likely contact you during those hours, lay the law down beforehand! (You could also set up "Do Not Disturb" hours on your laptop.)

5) Website blockers. Consider a browser extension or app (like SelfControl or StayFocused) that blocks access to certain websites during specific times. This strategy helps me avoid the rabbit hole of clicking links that I know will lead to a colossal time-suck.

6) Give yourself breaks. Breaks can assist your brain in resetting and refocusing on the task at hand. Revisit #14, "The Pomodoro Technique," or create your own method based on that.

The bottom line is that distractions can be controlled, but you've got to be proactive. Pinpoint those suckers and ruthlessly block them out.

#24: THE ART OF NOT MULTITASKING

Society has this glamorous idea of multitasking. We're led to believe it's a valuable skill - one of the "traits of successful people." As a result, our egoic minds tend to regard multi-tasking as some "badge of honor." We think the more jobs we can juggle at once, the better. "Look at me! I'm handling eight things at the same time! I'm amazing!" Well, ego - you're not an octopus, and you're not being amazing. You're actually being counterproductive.

Multitasking has *repeatedly* been shown to be less effective than focusing on one thing at a time. What seems like multi-tasking at the outset is really just the brain switching back and forth between tasks. This subtle waste of time makes completing everything take *longer* and degrades our work's **quality**. Not only that, but when done frequently enough, multitasking can deteriorate our attention span, cause burnout, and sometimes even lead to depression (Daugherty 2023).

You've more than likely heard the phrase, *"You cannot serve two masters."* Or how about *"If you chase two rabbits, you will not catch either"*? Although these phrases have broader mean-ings, they are still applicable here!

I'm not about to go into the science of this. It's kind of boring, to be honest. A simple Google search will prove why you don't need to juggle tasks but instead become laser-focused on **one thing at a time.**

Want to know how to apply your laser focus? Read on, my pupil...

#25: THE 80/20 RULE

I want to wrap this section up by introducing you to the highly effective "80/20 rule." It may be challenging to wrap your head around at first, but once it clicks, you'll realize that you can utilize it to study faster and get better grades - plus MUCH more.

It originated by Italian economist Vilfredo Pareto (I wonder if he knew the Pomodoro guy?) to explain the unequal distribution of wealth in Italy: he noticed that 20% of the population owned 80% of the land. The rule has since been used in various industries and recently entered the personal productivity space. Although not always exact, this rule is undoubtedly a phenomenon that has been observed all over the place.

The 80/20 rule, or Pareto principle, says that 80% of your results come from only 20% of your efforts. So, to maximize your results, **focus on the 20% yielding the most results** - and you will get the biggest bang for your buck.

This is especially important in high school when you have so much to do in so little time. Choosing which activities and tasks are *worth* your time can make all the difference.

It might be easiest to grasp this principle by looking at some everyday examples:

- You probably wear about 20% of all your clothes *most* of the time (perhaps, 80% of the time?).
- You probably have favorite books and movies that you watch or read more than others. The same goes for hobbies, sports, and activities – you'll always gravitate towards doing a *few* of them most often.
- You may find that out of all the people you interact with, you devote most of your time to just a handful of them.
- 80% of a restaurant's orders typically come from 20% or fewer menu items.
- 20% of employees often generate 80% of a company's profits.
- 20% of criminals commit 80% of crimes.
- 20% of athletes result in 80% of points scored.

Let's simplify it and remove the exact ratio: from now on, attempt to *spend most of your time on the things that matter*. That's it. The 80/20 rule is ultimately a lesson in **efficiency**.

As I mentioned, we can specifically apply it here to studying:

- If you're reading a book for research, often you can more or less skim the chapters that don't matter and focus on the ones that do (depending on the type of reading or project - use your discretion here).
- If you're studying for a test, highlight the key points instead of memorizing every single word on your notes.

- If you're choosing between classes, prioritize and pick the ones most aligned with where you want to go in life.
- Spend more time on activities that align with your interests and career goals.

You may already be doing this to a degree. You may even find it's more or less "common sense." But with this technique especially, knowing the science behind it can help you "internalize" and implement it to **higher** degrees.

It's important to remember that you're looking for productivity - not perfection - in your teens. The goal should be to learn the material, make progress, meet your objectives, and get the most out of your high school experience - not to be a robot.

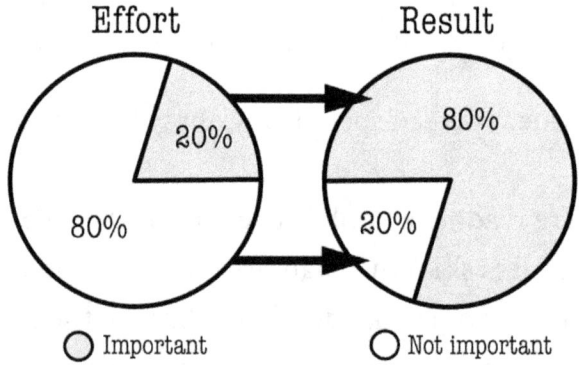

This rule may take some finesse and time to master. As you get better at it, you'll turn an hour's worth of studying into about 12 or 13 minutes. You'll start instinctively knowing what to focus on, which will inevitably help you maximize your results and be more successful. Don't be surprised if the 80/20 rule pops up again!

3

RELATIONSHIPS

"Our rewards in life will always be in exact proportion to the amount of consideration we show toward others."

— EARL NIGHTINGALE

From the day we are born till the day we die, the relationships we form will be the foundations of our lives. Relationships show us how to handle our successes and failures. They help shape our character. They teach us empathy and compassion. And they give us the sense of belonging and connection we so badly crave and need as human beings.

I'll admit something: I was a little punk as a kid. I constantly fought with my mother, challenged my father's authority, and borderline tortured my brother (don't worry, I grew up). You would be wise to learn from my mistakes!

Relationships with parents, teachers, friends, partners, and relatives are essential building blocks for a successful and happy life. However, navigating the complexities of these relationships during adolescence can be a challenge. We might feel overwhelmed by the unknowns or misunderstood by those closest to us. And, as I've discovered, it often takes far too long to realize that our ***relationships are worth more than gold***.

As guiding principles throughout this section, I urge you to remember two things:

1) You must never take your loved ones for granted. Remember that these connections are priceless and irreplaceable. Trust me; you don't want to come to this conclusion when it's too late - when you have to face the fact that you should've done things differently...And **2)** The people in your life are a reflection of **you**. The good, the bad, and everything in between. It is entirely up to you how much effort and attention you devote to each relationship. YOU choose how you show up for others and how much respect and care you give back. Remember this power!

I hope the upcoming information helps you become more aware and intentional with those you care about. Because through them, you'll be able to understand *yourself* better and recognize what is truly important. I hope you learn to honor and strengthen your relationships, forming mutually beneficial, life-affirming, and lifelong commitments.

NOTE: This section might come across as less "hacky" and more just, really good advice. Just go with it.

HACK #26: LIVE FROM THE INSIDE OUT (SELF)

"How you love yourself is how you teach others to love you."

— RUPI KAUR

When you begin to internalize the importance of relationships, you will eventually realize that YOU are the pumping heart of each one. I firmly believe that we cannot give others what we don't already have in ourselves. Therefore, we need to make the relationship with ourselves number ONE.

Without self-love, you will unknowingly and unconsciously sabotage every relationship you have from the very start. You will look to others to fill voids or assign blame, often draining their energy and harming them (and yourself).

On the other hand, when you love yourself, a strong force emerges that enables you to honestly care for and connect with others without *any* expectations or judgment. It is the realization that your happiness comes from **within** rather than from **without**. It is the acceptance of who you are *exactly* as you are - and who your loved ones are exactly as *they* are.

Yes, you must learn to love yourself. Forgive yourself. Be patient with yourself. KNOW yourself.

My book *"Building Unstoppable Self-Confidence for Teens"* is **all** about this. If you struggle with self-esteem, I highly recommend reading that book. It goes in-depth on:

- Finding yourself
- How to think
- Discovering your passions
- Loving your body
- Creating boundaries
- Choosing influencers
- Living boldly

Since SO much more is involved on this topic, the complete hack #26 would be: *read my last book!*

But until then, start internalizing this fact: **you are the nucleus of every relationship in your life.**

#27: BEFRIEND YOUR PARENTS (PARENTS)

What it's not: Becoming their BEST friend. Treating them like one of your "buddies" or forgetting that they are your parents. Disregarding their authority and decision-making.

What it is: Being receptive to their experience and wisdom, even if you don't agree with or understand it at the time. Establishing a friendly and respectful relationship with them. Keeping the lines of communication open and remembering that they were once young, just like you.

Now, I understand that there are two camps out there. One preaches that parents should not be "friends" with their kids - that they should portray authority figures and that the relationship should remain strictly hierarchical or disciplinary. Then you have the other end of the spectrum - where parents and teens are so close that they almost become like siblings - overly casual and relaxed.

Here's the thing: neither of these extremes will likely foster an emotionally healthy relationship between you and your parent. However, it is possible to both respect AND befriend your parents.

Understand that I'm suggesting *you* view THEM as a friend. But remember that it is *their* job and obligation to be your **parents**. And despite any current differences, they (should...hopefully!) ultimately want what's best for you.

In getting the most from this standpoint, here are the aspects of friendship that WILL work:

- Being honest
- Talking to them about anything - big or small, serious or silly
- Listening to their advice with an open heart and mind
- Showing respect at all times - even when it's hard
- Apologizing and owning your mistakes
- Supporting each other when there are challenges
- Laughing together and having fun

The floodgates will open up if these are implemented with respect and good intention. This is when you'll realize how your newfound wisdom puts you much farther than others who don't quite "get it" yet. Now you'll be going *with* the flow rather than fighting against it. Some fantastic benefits may include the following:

- MORE FREEDOM (this alone will be worth it)
- An increased sense of safety and knowing that someone always has your back, even when you make mistakes
- More guidance and support in life decisions
- Improved communication skills, as you learn to listen better and express yourself

- Improved relationships with *others* as you hone your skills at home
- Greater expansion of self, as you will be treated more and more like an adult
- Greater appreciation for family and understanding of unconditional love

Amen.

#28: THE CODE WORD (PARENTS)

When I was about ten years old, my mother created a "code word" with me (actually, it was two rhyming words). This code was very sacred; only she and I knew what it was (I believe she even had a separate one with my brother). It was a word to be used **strictly** for emergencies - if she or I were in trouble.

Let me give you an example. Say I was walking home from school one day or to the bus, and an adult I didn't know approached me. Suppose they said something like, "Hey, Derek! I'm a friend of your mother - she had an accident and got rushed to the ER. She asked me if I would pick you up and bring you to her so you wouldn't be home alone." As a kid, I might not know what to do, questioning: "Should I believe this person I don't know? What if this is true, and my mom *does* need me right now?"

That's when I would ask them what the **code word** was. I would know that in a case such as this, my mother would have entrusted this person with the password that *only* the two of us knew - and that I could safely get in the car with them. Luckily, we never had to use it.

There could be many other uses for a code word between you and your parent(s). Get creative! Not only will it increase your safety, but it can form a special bond.

Are you wondering what our code word was? It was very quirky; I still remember it to this day. And no, I will not tell you what it is. Ironically, I asked my mom last year if she remembered it - and she forgot! Good thing I'm an adult now.

#29: PULL THE AWKWARD CONVO BAND-AID OFF QUICKLY (PARENTS)

As we navigate adolescence's uncharted territory, we find that the good old, classic "awkward conversation" is inevitable. Puberty, sex, relationships, health issues, drugs & alcohol, religion & spirituality - I'm starting to feel awkward just writing about it. I'm about to pull the band-aid off this *hack* real fast!

And yeah, this one IS a hack. Because these conversations are unavoidable doesn't mean they must be drawn out and *painful*. So, once you know there's something awkward to be discussed, follow these two rules:

1) Pick a good time to approach your parent(s), use your **feelings** to lead the conversation, and rip that band-aid right off. For instance: "I'm worried how you might react, but *blank*." Or, "This is embarrassing, but I kind of need to talk to you about *blank*." This WILL feel uncomfortable at first – like jumping into cold water. But now the band-aid is off. And, like jumping into cold water, your body will soon acclimate to the temperature.

2) The real key is consistent practice. See, having **one** awkward convo and then shying away from that sort of thing again makes it equally (or more) uncomfortable the next time. It *becomes* an embarrassing thing because it's so rare. Therefore, both parties will continue to feel weird about it. What you want to do is **normalize** these conversations. Bring up every little embarrassing thing you want to - keep that door open! Make it so familiar that no one even *bats an eye* at it anymore. You might notice that it even becomes charmingly funny (in a serious-talk kind of way)!

The benefit is that you'll take the elephant in the room and turn him into a cute little bunny. When the more significant conversations come along (like college, money, relationships, etc.), you won't be *nearly* as intimidated by them - that stuff will be a breeze.

#30: THE CODE PHRASE (PARENTS/FRIENDS)

While the code *word* can **protect** you against dangerous situations, a code *phrase* can be implemented to **remove** you from embarrassing, harmful, or hazardous situations. The best way to explain this might be through another example.

Context: You're at a house party, but the wrong kind of people show up, and you find yourself in an uncomfortable situation.

Maybe they have alcohol or drugs. Perhaps they are known for starting fights. Or, you just get an overall *bad vibe* from these people. Whatever the reason, it doesn't feel right - and you want OUT. That's when you text the code phrase.

When establishing this phrase with your parents, you should make it **very specific**. It needs to be a message without confusion as to what it means, yet, it should be natural-sounding. That way, it becomes "camouflaged," and no one snooping over your shoulder will know the better. For instance, "Will you check and make sure I turned off the light in my room?" Or, "Don't forget to feed the dog tonight!" The point is that when your parent receives the text, they'll *know* it's a signal to get you out of there ASAP.

The next part of this plan is that your parent will call your phone - this will act as your alibi. A preset "emergency" will be the reason you have to leave the party (again, establish the specific details of the "emergency" ahead of time). As far as your peers go, there's no need for further explanation. No one judges you for leaving because it looks legit. As far as your parents go, they're at ease knowing you're now safe and did the right thing. (Attaching a "no questions asked" clause to the code phrase can be very beneficial. That way, you *and* your parents feel comfortable, and you don't have to disclose details unless you want to.)

A code phrase can also be used with your best friends - but leave the serious situations to adults. Friends could aid in getting you away from an argument, a boring conversation, or any other uncomfortable social situation at school which doesn't warrant parental intervention. Feel free to use your creativity and imagination - just keep it moral and ethical, please! The whole purpose of the code phrase is to protect the greatest good of all parties involved.

#31: "L.E.E.H.A." – THE FIVE QUALITIES OF A TRUE FRIEND (FRIENDS)

Real friendship is a beautiful thing. It's fulfilling, meaningful, fun, and rewarding. If you've ever experienced a moment when you truly needed a friend - and one was there for you - then you know what I mean. That said, *being* a great friend is just as important or even more important than *having* one. If you practice and develop these five qualities, you will put yourself in a position to maintain unstoppable, lasting bonds with your friends.

1) Loyalty. One of the cornerstones of friendship. It's the ability to be there through thick and thin, even when it may not make sense. It includes being trustworthy and someone who can be confidently confided in.

2) Equality. This often gets overlooked. Both sides should feel respected and valued. Keep yourself from becoming so preoccupied with your own wants and needs that you lose sight of *balance*; for instance, talking over the other person or constantly asserting yourself.

3) Empathy. The ability to relate to *how* and *why* a person feels the way they do. Empathy is caring and connecting on a personal level. This deep compassion is a gift that sometimes only a **best** friend can give.

4) Honesty. Another cornerstone. Learn to develop openness and sincerity in your words and interactions, whether positive or negative, big or small. A lack of honesty can be the downfall of any friendship.

5) Accountability. A true friend holds not only themselves but the *other* person accountable. It requires a bit of tough love, but never in a cruel or demeaning way. This ability to challenge and "push to be better" without degradation will cause the relationship AND the individuals to grow. You become like a machine that works to improve all sides.

#32: THE ART OF LETTING PEOPLE GO (FRIENDS)

If you read my previous book, you'll know that after switching school systems in seventh grade, I dealt with a few years of harsh bullying. Luckily when high school began, it finally started to let up. For some reason, one of the most popular kids in my grade, Bryan, decided he was "cool with me." I didn't question why! In some ways, he was a lifesaver.

I can't really call it a friendship, but this "association" definitely had its perks: no one messed with me anymore. Other popular kids began to notice me. And the whole thing made me feel good about myself.

But deep down inside, I knew this wasn't real - it was more of a novelty. I always felt trapped under his thumb, like I had to be the person he wanted me to be. On top of that, his friend group was into things that were...questionable, at best. I realized I was perpetuating the situation because it benefited my social status and not because of a genuine, mutual relationship. As time went on, I knew I had to let him go.

You may have experienced a toxic relationship like this - and if not, you will. Whether it be a friend, acquaintance, boyfriend/girlfriend, or in extreme cases, family - sometimes you have to make the tough decision to **let people go** in order to **grow**. But it's certainly not that easy.

Here are some tips to make this process a little smoother for you:

1) Know your "why." Get very clear on your reasons for letting this person go. How does the relationship affect you now, and how could it affect you in the long run? Can you do anything to make the relationship healthier, or is it just time to cut the cord? If it feels toxic or anything less than mutually beneficial, then it's probably time to part ways.

2) Prepare yourself. Depending on the degree of toxicity, you may need to brace yourself for a difficult conversation. It can help to rehearse the worst possible outcome mentally. That might sound dark, but chances are that the worst-case scenario is *not* likely. If you are prepared for it, any other result will seem much easier to handle.

3) Utilize your support system. Sometimes decisions like this can feel all-consuming, causing us to live in our minds and close ourselves off from the great relationships we *do* have. Including friends or parents in your plan can be very, very comforting. And if it *does* go down the "worst-case scenario" path this time, your loved ones will be on the same page and ready to provide the support you need.

4) Have "the conversation." Think beforehand about what you want to say and how you plan on saying it. There is no need to lie - be honest and direct. Deliver your message, but do it with kindness and compassion, making it clear that this is not a personal attack on them. If the conversation escalates, and if necessary, express that you are not open to any debate. Remember: you have the right to choose who stays in your life.

5) Don't burn bridges - part ways with respect. Whatever the circumstance, there's always value in gracefully exiting an unhealthy relationship - not only for *your* mental health but *theirs*. Leave the door open for potential reconciliation in the future. Try not to think of others as "bad" but rather as being at a different point in their journey than you are.

As you may discover, letting people go can get messy. Follow these guidelines, but keep in mind that the "art" of it comes with experience and learning to adapt to each individual and specific situation.

#33: THE SMALL CIRCLE (FRIENDS)

This piece of advice goes hand in hand with the art of letting people go.

We *all* want to be known as "popular" at some point. We all want people to like us, and we all want to be accepted. But this innate desire can be somewhat blinding. Don't be fooled into thinking that *quantity* is more important than **quality** - it's not! Although there are many advantages to keeping your friend circle small, it mostly comes down to two significant benefits:

1) Keeping out the "noise." You are less likely to attract the *wrong* type of people into your life when you don't keep an overly large friend group. It's commonly stated that you are "the average of the five people you spend the most time with." In other words, *we tend to adopt the traits of those with whom we spend the most time.* On top of that, as your friend circle grows, so does your risk of meeting people who don't have your best interests at heart. These people can drain your energy, manipulate your emotions, and take advantage of you. I'm not saying that everyone outside your small circle is bad; far from it. I'm saying that the more people you have around you, the harder it is to *determine* who truly has your best interests at heart, the less time you have for the people and things that truly matter, and the more opinions, influences, and "noise" you have to filter through daily. To put it bluntly: fewer friends equals less drama.

2) Keeping close bonds. When you have a small friend circle, your relationships will be stronger. You are now focusing on a few special friendships rather than being spread thinly across many. A meaningful level of intimacy can only be achieved by investing in a closed, secure support system. This is why the connections you form within your smaller group are so valuable. You get to know each other on a deeper level - you understand each other's struggles and successes, you support one another through thick and thin, and you can be vulnerable with one another in ways that would be dangerous with strangers or acquaintances. You'll also feel less like you're missing out on things (a nice bonus) because you'll have fewer people to worry about.

Even if this goes against what you might assume, consider taking a leap of faith here and trusting what so many before you have come to learn:

"As I get older, I am becoming more selective of who I consider a friend. I find that I would rather have 4 quarters than 100 pennies."

— STEVE MARABOLI

"The faker you are, the bigger your circle will be. The realer you are, the smaller your circle will be."

— RYAN REYNOLDS

"There are over 7 billion people in this world. I like 6 of you."

— UNKNOWN

#34: YOUR DATING BAROMETER (DATING)

When is it time to start dating? How do you know when you're ready? Like, *really* ready - not just going by the status quo. Are you too young? Or maybe your friends are starting to date, and for some reason, you just aren't feeling it yet?

Because the answers to these questions vary across individuals, there is more than one answer. There are invariably many factors to consider. However, one thing is for sure: your answer needs to be tailored to *you*. Fortunately, that part is very, very easy.

The description of a barometer in the dictionary is *"a scientific instrument for measuring atmospheric pressure, also called barometric pressure."* But to use your dating barometer, you don't have to know anything about science. You only need to know one word from that description - **pressure**.

Let "pressure" become your instrument for measuring your readiness. When faced with a decision or thoughts about entering into a relationship, ask yourself: "Am I feeling any outside pressure?" As soon as you ask, and as surely as the sun rises every morning, your instinct will *immediately* give you the correct answer (I told you this was easy). And it's that **first answer** you want to go with - before your rational mind kicks in and tries to persuade you otherwise. Simply put, if you are feeling *any* pressure, it's not time to date - it isn't right yet. Dating is a very sensitive, multi-faceted dynamic that involves more than one person's feelings - and it gets more delicate the younger you are.

That being said, remember that this is just the first step. There is undoubtedly such a thing as dating too young (even if you feel you are ready), in which case you should consult with your parents, as there are alternatives such as group dating. Just never, EVER conform to *outside pressure* to date (or to do anything, really). Never go against your barometer.

#35: RED-FLAG DESPERATION (DATING)

Like pressure, "desperation" should be another word you become keenly aware of when stepping into the dating ring. You should red-flag a situation **99% of the time** if you sense: urgency, strain, or even anxiety in the desire to find someone special as soon as possible. It's the sensation of being *so* needy for connection that one is willing to accept anything and anyone who comes along. Desperation should be flagged when you feel it from others AND when sensed in yourself!

This emotion or feeling is hazardous because it can lead to bad decisions and unhealthy relationships. It's important to remember that *your worth is not dependent on having another person in your life.* You don't need someone to "complete" you or validate your existence. Regardless of your relationship status, you are more than valuable and worthy.

Sometimes it's not easy to sense the desperation in yourself or another because infatuation tends to be blinding (think heart-eyes emoji). Therefore, keep a lookout for these behaviors:

- Becoming *way* too involved *way* too soon (or overly clingy)
- Needing to know each other's whereabouts at all times
- Constantly sacrificing time with family, friends, and loved ones
- Excessive spending on clothes, hairstyles, accessories, and other image-related items to appear more appealing to one specific person
- Constantly checking messages and jumping whenever a phone buzzes or vibrates
- Going through another's personal items (phone/backpack/purse/room)
- Extreme sensitivity and jealousy
- Being too physical or sexual when it's not the time or place

The truth is that if we let it, desperation can lead us down an extremely dark path. Early in any relationship, it's critical to establish boundaries and standards. It is your responsibility as a young adult to recognize warning signs before they become *fatal errors*. Take time to reflect on what truly matters, and remember that **you can always choose differently.**

#36: DON'T ADULT YET (DATING)

What it's not: "I don't have to take too much responsibility for myself because I'm not an adult yet." "Since I'm not a grown-up, I can be promiscuous and fool around." "When I'm older, I'll worry more about other peoples' feelings - but for now, we're just kids, so it's not a big deal."

What it is: You don't get to make up your own translation as to what I mean when saying, "Don't adult yet," ok? #36 concerns **acting** like an adult in a dating scenario when you are *not* one yet. Emphasis on "ACTING"! I'll make it crystal clear for you. Follow this list of "*What not to do,*" and you'll know exactly what I'm talking about:

- Don't profess your undying love and make over-the-top commitments.
- Don't act hyper-serious, like the two of you are the stars of some romance/drama/thriller, and all that matters is your love.
- Don't try and convince your love interest of "how mature" you are.
- Don't give and show off hickeys (cringe).
- Don't talk about your future together in fantastical ways while abandoning the present.
- Don't expect to get married or have your "own family" anytime soon.
- Don't have long make-out sessions in public.
- Don't be attached at the hip.

- Don't sacrifice your friends and family (sounds like desperation...).
- Aside from maybe prom, don't dress up to the nines and go on fancy one-on-one dates.

Picking up what I'm putting down? Ultimately, try to understand that you aren't ready to be overly romantic just yet. Adult *actions* require adult *responsibility* and result in adult *consequences*. Read that again! Our brains don't even finish developing until well into our twenties. So, take some time and focus on getting to know each other, getting to know yourself, and having *responsible* fun together.

#37: OK, NOW YOU CAN ADULT (DATING)

Bear with me - this is the last bit on dating. I know there are lots of swirling feelings going on throughout these years. I know how intense things seem. But if you trust in this advice, I promise it will help navigate you.

Can you guess at what point it's time to act like an adult when it comes to dating? It's at the part which hurts the most, the very end: **breaking up**.

No teen escapes the heartache of breakups. And when you look at it objectively, it only makes sense: teens are relatively young. There is much growing to do, so it's normal to grow apart, change, or not get along anymore. But as you know by now, just because something might be "normal" doesn't mean it won't hurt like a punch to the gut. Depending on who's dumping who, or even if it's mutual, there will undoubtedly be *mixed feelings* that can add to this cocktail of sorrow.

It's precisely because these times can be so emotionally volatile that you can't afford *not* to act like an adult. This is your time to step up. If you want to play the dating game, you must learn how to break up gracefully.

With that, I leave you with the "dos and don'ts" of breaking up:

DO

...it in person. Don't break up over a text, phone call, or email (if possible).

...it if it's right for you - even if you know it will hurt the other person. Know that it will be worse if it's dragged out.

...be completely honest, but don't say anything harsh you might regret. Show respect and empathy for the other person's feelings.

...ask for help or advice from parents, older siblings, or mature-enough friends if you need to.

...understand that it's painful for **both** sides. This can be hard to swallow if you're on the "receiving" end.

DON'T

...coward out and ghost the person you're breaking up with.

...put it off. Again, dragging it out makes things harder for both people. You also create space for the other person to hear about it from someone else - this can be *devastating*.

...play the blame game. No need to point fingers or accuse each other.

...give false hope. Don't say, "Let's be friends" or "Maybe we'll get back together" if you know you don't mean it.

...run your mouth. Being an adult means keeping personal things personal and honoring another's privacy. The whole school doesn't need to know your ex cried over you for three hours last night.

...use someone new as a distraction. Avoid jumping into another relationship before you've had time to process the feelings of your past one.

And remember: when one door closes, another one opens. It's probably a DoorDash delivery guy with your favorite comfort food. But eventually, it will be someone very special. You have *tons* of time to find this someone, but you only have one life - so don't rush it! When the right person comes along, it will make perfect sense why you needed this life experience.

#38: COMMUNICATE C-L-E-A-R-L-Y (ALL)

To wrap up "Relationships," I want to leave you with three concise and practical techniques to benefit *every single one* of yours. The first of the three is **clear communication**.

We've come full circle to "everything starts with you." This is because you must first know what YOU want to be clear with others. Determining what you want, need, and feel may take time and effort. But communicating these things will be far more manageable once you have clarity. This shows enormous amounts of mental maturity!

Being concise rather than vague *prevents confusion and promotes mutual understanding*. This is the ultimate goal of communication - to understand each other. Think about when you're ordering at a restaurant. You don't say to the server, "I'll have something warm, please." Or "Just give me something that will fill me up." You could very well end up with a pile of flavorless, overcooked rice. Instead, you order precisely: "I'll have the grilled salmon with a side of steamed broccoli and roasted potatoes." This ensures you get *exactly* what you desire.

A story that illustrates the importance of clearly speaking comes from my friend's embarrassing teen-dating experience. He went to pick up his girlfriend from her house one day, and her father answered the door. The dad was very blunt and opened with, "What do *you* want?" My friend replied with a confused look: "Ummm...your daughter?"

Needless to say, her dad didn't like that answer and made it known. A better first impression might've been made if my friend said something like, "Hello sir, my name is *blank*, and I'm here to pick up your daughter for a movie at 7:10 - if that's all right?"

When someone asks you a question, do you sometimes find it easier to be vague with your response? For instance, when I ask my kids how school was, I can safely bet nine out of ten times that the answer will be "...good" (we're working on that). A lazy, unclear response could mean you never get help with that tough assignment, a bully, or the joy of expressing something significant that happened.

It's not *only* about projecting clearly - communication is a two-way street. Get in the habit of **listening** clearly to what the other person is trying to convey, too. This will heighten respect levels, deliver desired outcomes, and improve your relationships in general.

#39: DON'T USE THEM WRONG (ALL)

Sometimes all it takes to transform your relationships for the better is simply adjusting how you view them.

I'm going to take a page from my own book (pun definitely intended) and communicate very clearly here:

It is not your responsibility to control people.

It is not your place to tell someone else how to live their life.

It is not your right to pass judgment on or criticize others.

People should not be used as tools or a means to an end.

Respect your relationships, and treat them with the same kindness and care you'd want in return. Our only control is that of *ourselves* - when you accept that responsibility and do the internal work, you will see all your relationships blossom. If you ever catch yourself "using" someone else for personal gain - even if you don't *think* it's affecting them negatively - I advise you to pause, take a step back, and evaluate your true intentions.

#40: ADMIT YOU'RE WRONG (ALL)

Admitting when you're wrong can be one of the hardest things for people to do. Nobody likes to look like a fool, accept defeat, or appear weak. However, having the humility to admit and apologize when you make a mistake is a vital life skill that can benefit your relationships (and self-esteem) in the long run.

There's no need to get into the science of it - just know that admitting you're wrong is one of the most *healing, liberating, and humbling experiences you can have*. It demonstrates a deep respect for yourself and others, makes peace with the fact that we all make mistakes, and provides an opportunity to start over and **build bridges instead of walls**.

For the sake of your loved ones, learn to embrace the power of an apology. Get used to saying "I'm sorry" and, more importantly, *meaning* it. Don't let your subconscious accumulate feelings of pride or shame. The last thing the ego needs is to be fed. Acknowledge your errors, learn from them, and ultimately accept responsibility for your actions.

To end on a cliché: admitting you're wrong is not a sign of weakness, but rather a strength of character. And unlike the ego, character is a good thing to feed. I'd avoid feeding it the overcooked rice, though.

4

HEALTH & HOME

"My favorite way of getting out of doing chores is by acting like I'm asleep. But it never works."

— DEVON WERKHEISER

I like this bouncing back and forth from philosophical to practical. And since the last section was more philosophical, onward with the practical hacks! This chapter will be fun and to the point.

If you're going to master adulting before it masters you, then you **must** become a master of your health and home. I plan to deliver fresh and unique tips to avoid boring you with the same nutrition, hygiene, and cleaning advice you've heard a million times. Enjoy these game-changing strategies that will help you optimize your living conditions in fun ways and yield *actual* results.

HACK #41: MASTER THE MICROWAVE

My mother would freak out if she thought I was promoting this "radiation machine"! Well, I have two things to say: 1) Some people grossly exaggerate the perceived "harmful effects" of microwaves. In fact, there is no evidence showing that they are even dangerous at all (Tolliver 2021). 2) I am not *promoting* microwaves, per se. If you know how to cook without one, more power to you.

But let's face it: as a young adult, you won't have time to cook every meal. You won't have the money to buy every meal. And other people won't always be there to prepare food for you. Inevitably, you're going to end up microwaving stuff. I'm just here to help you get the most out of this "non-ionizing (safe) radiation machine." And so, I bring you *the ultimate microwave hacks*:

1) Ripen bananas. If you aren't trying to explode the banana, poke some holes in it first. Then pop it in for 15 seconds at a time until it's ripe or soft enough.

2) Get the most out of a lemon. Microwave your citrus for 15-20 seconds, roll it on the counter a few times, cut it in half, then *squeeze* to get the maximum amount of juice out.

3) Hot dog express (a personal favorite). Dampen a paper towel and wrap a hot dog or two in it. Microwave for 30 seconds to a minute. Way faster than boiling!

4) Soften ice cream. For those of you who (like me) do not enjoy hard ice cream OR waiting for it to soften. Heat it in 10-second intervals until it's at your perfectly desired level of softness.

5) Scrambled eggs. Crack the eggs into a bowl and add a drop of milk, salt, and pepper to your liking. Whisk them up with a fork, then microwave for roughly 40 seconds, stirring every 10-15 seconds.

6) Make a latte. Fill a glass jar (or something microwavable with a lid) with milk. Nuke it for about a minute or until it's hot. Put the top on and shake it for about 15 seconds. Pour into a mug with some coffee or espresso, and you'll get a fancy foamy drink.

7) Bring back bread. Have some stale bread that you'd still like to use? As with the hot dogs, wrap the bread in a damp paper towel. Microwave for only about 10 seconds to soften it.

8) Baked potato. Poke some holes in your potato with a fork to vent. Microwave for six to seven minutes, then slice it open and give it some butter, cheese, sour cream, salt, and pepper. This takes slightly longer than the others but is still quicker than the oven.

9) Quesadilla. Put a tortilla on a microwave-safe plate, then top it with cheese and any other desired ingredients. Now you can cover it with another tortilla (large) or fold it in half (small). Microwave for about 20 seconds, flip the quesadilla over, and microwave for an additional 10-20 seconds or until the cheese melts. Quick, easy, and delicious.

10) Steamed veggies. Put your veggies in a microwavable bowl, add a tablespoon or two of water, and cover with a microwavable plate - heat for three to four minutes or until the desired doneness.

Ramen. If you don't know how to make ramen, are you even a teenager?

Bonus: What NOT to put in the microwave - ever. *Tinfoil. Metal. Styrofoam. Paper bags. Plastic bags or containers. Hot peppers. Eggs with the shell. Toys. Pets.*

#42: FIVE 5-MINUTE RECIPES

There are countless recipes out there, and I don't want to turn this into a cookbook. But I *do* want to provide something useful on the topic besides microwaving bananas and hot dogs.

These meals are intended to be fast and easy, with just a few ingredients and even less prep time. They're great when you're in a rush or don't want to spend hours in the kitchen.

Recipes like these can be found all over the internet, but I've compiled a few of my favorites here.

1) PB&J Smoothie: This smoothie only requires three ingredients - peanut butter, jelly, and yogurt - blended for about 30 seconds. It's simple, healthy, and portable!

2) Avocado Toast: You'll need one ripe avocado, olive oil, and two slices of toast to make this delectable breakfast or snack. Cut the avocado down the center and split it to remove the pit. Scoop out the insides of each half and mash them with a fork in a bowl. Spread this mixture onto each piece of toast and then drizzle with olive oil.

3) Gourmet Grilled Cheese: ...or plain old grilled cheese. All you need for the plain version is two slices of cheese, two slices of bread, and some butter. Put butter on one side of each piece of bread, then grill them on a skillet with butter side down. Place your cheese slices on top of the bread and cook until heated through and the cheese is melted. Now, flip one piece of bread over the other (the outside should be golden brown). Make it "gourmet" by getting creative and adding other ingredients like tomatoes, onions, bacon, spinach, or whatever else you can find in the fridge...

4) Egg in a Hole: A quick and easy breakfast option that requires just four ingredients - an egg, butter, bread, and seasonings of your choice. Start by cutting a hole in the middle of a slice of bread using a biscuit cutter, the rim of a glass, or even a knife. Melt some butter in a skillet over medium heat, then put the bread in. Crack the egg into the hole and season with salt and pepper. Cook until the egg whites are firm, then flip it over to cook the other side.

5) Loaded Nachos: ...or plain nachos. This delicious and satisfying snack or light meal requires minimal effort. To make it, layer your favorite tortilla chips onto an oven-safe dish. Top them with grated cheese - and leave it at that if you like them plain (like my strange son). Otherwise, you can add cooked ground beef or chicken, refried beans, diced tomatoes, onions, jalapenos, sliced olives, or anything else your little heart desires. Pop it in the oven for a few minutes until the cheese melts and everything is heated through. They're done! Now don't skimp on the sour cream and salsa.

As I said, these are just a few of my quick go-to's. Admittedly, the kitchen has never really been my strong suit. But if cooking excites you, I encourage you to find and perfect some more recipes and add your own twist! Cooking will score you *major* points in many areas down the road.

#43: PREP FOR SUCCESS

As we wrap things up in the kitchen, I'd like to provide you with the **master keys** for cooking *anything* and *everything*. If you set these tactics in place, it doesn't matter how simple or complicated the recipe is - half the battle will already be won. And yes, I realize I disclosed my cooking incompetence just a few minutes ago. So, you can rest assured that I did my research here and that this stuff is legit. I'm even feeling inspired to see what I can whip up now...

1) Read the entire recipe first. Get an idea of the timeline, ingredients, and steps involved before you dig in - even pull out the utensils, pots, and pans you'll need.

2) Clear the sink. A clear workspace equals a clear mind. Plus, your flow will be nice and smooth when it comes time to rinse or wash something.

3) Secure your cutting board. Place your cutting board on top of a damp kitchen towel - this will help keep it from sliding around and prevent accidents.

4) Start prepping. Wash, chop, dice, slice - do whatever needs to be done before the actual cooking starts. At this stage, you'll also want to preheat the oven (if necessary).

5) Grab a large bowl for waste. Put your scraps, peelings, and other trash in there. This will help keep the counter clear and save multiple trips to the trash can.

6) Turn on some tunes. An optional suggestion! And one more piece of personal advice from the little cooking I *have* done? *Clean as you go.*

Now, go forth and master-chef it up!

***If things don't turn out as planned, remember that it's all part of the learning process. Like everything else, this will get easier over time. Take a breath, try again tomorrow, and enjoy the

> *adventure. It's okay to make mistakes - that's how we get better.****

#44: LINKING LAUNDRY

The more I write and research, the more I realize I should follow my own advice. And that this book isn't *just* for teens.

That's because I constantly lose socks in the laundry, or pairs constantly get separated between loads. This trick is so obvious that it should be common sense, yet most of us probably don't do it. It involves tying together anything that comes in pairs - socks, mittens, gloves, slippers, etc. They'll never lose each other if you bind them with a rubber or hair band or even tie them together.

This also goes for hoodie strings and drawstrings on pants - take a few seconds to knot them loosely before they go into the dirty pile. Nothing is more frustrating than having a hoodie string pulled out in the wash.

Bonus: For those times that you do lose a hoodie or pants string, there is a simple solution. Secure one end of the string to a paper clip or a pen with a pocket clip (I prefer a pen because it's longer). Feeding the pen through the hole in your hoodie or pants will allow you to pull the string back through easily and is way quicker than inch-worming that thing for 10 minutes.

#45: TOUCH TEN

Cleaning can be a daunting task. I haven't met too many people who enjoy cleaning, although they do exist. Regardless, it's a necessary "evil" that you must learn to deal with. And guess what? Your parents won't be cleaning up after you for the rest of your life - or even, like, the rest of your teen years.

The "Touch Ten" technique is a simple way of making steady progress without becoming overwhelmed. Take your messy room, for example. Every day, touch ten things - no more, no less - that need to be either cleaned, moved, organized, or gotten rid of. Ten is a manageable number that shouldn't overload you. If you stick to doing this once a day, then over time, your room will look less like a pigsty and more like an apartment in the city. You might be amazed at how much progress this simple process brings you long-term.

#46: THE TOOTHBRUSH REVOLUTION

For too long, the humble toothbrush has taken a backseat to...well, basically everything outside of the oral-hygiene world. It does its morning and nightly routine and then fades into the background until it's time to brush again. It's sad, but you can't really *blame* it for being taken for granted. With a name like "toothbrush," what else are we supposed to expect from it?

I'm here today to let you know that this little magic wand has much more potential than we give it credit for. I believe its day has come - that it's the toothbrush's time to shine. Let me show you the ways...

- First of all, like a cat, your toothbrush has more than one life. Once the bristles start to fray, you might think it's time to send it off to the trash. Instead, try soaking it in hot water for half an hour to soften the bristles back up. Rub your thumb over them to release any debris. Then, rinse in cold water and air dry. Voila - it's new again! (I don't know that a toothbrush necessarily has nine lives, but it's good for at least two.)

Here are some other unique superpowers you might like to be aware of. Although, I recommend you don't use a toothbrush in these ways until it is, in fact, "dead" (for obvious reasons):

- Your toothbrush is excellent at cleaning off your electronic devices: your laptop keyboard, ports, speakers, and all the crevices of your cell phone - even the screen.
- It can scrub away stained grout in the bathroom, kitchen, and laundry areas.
- It can remove accumulated gunk in the showerhead, faucet handles, and other hard-to-reach places.

- It can clean your jewelry and eyeglasses.
- You can use it to apply hair dye...
- ...remove dirt from your fingernails...
- ...clean out your hairbrush...
- ...even use it as an eyebrow brush!

Now, what's that, you say? The toothbrush's sidekick, "toothpaste," also deserves its time in the sun? You're right. Toothpaste is great for many things outside dental hygiene - it can be used to clean jewelry and chrome easily and even remove stains from clothes. But my favorite thing about this trusty counterpart? *It fixes cracks on your phone screen and furniture.* Just dab some on, wipe it clean, and watch them cracks vanish. Who knew?

#47: BEFRIEND YOUR VINEGAR

Could white vinegar and its vast array of uses be considered "life-changing"? Well, it might not necessarily be ranked in the Top 10 of that category. But check it out - vinegar is **very** inexpensive. And it does have *many* uses - even more than the ones I'm about to present (I'm trying to keep it relevant here). Could you imagine how impressive it would be if one day you came to your parents like: "Oh - I have the perfect solution to this problem," went over to the cabinet, and whipped out a bottle of white vinegar? Also, you're going to be living on your own relatively soon. Since it virtually never expires, wouldn't it be a great idea to keep some vinegar at home, knowing what you could do with it? Yeah. I thought so.

1) Clean your clothes. *And make them smell better.* Run a cycle of clothes through the washing machine, adding about half a cup (or a cup, depending on the load size) of vinegar. This will soften the fabric, refresh the smell, AND brighten the colors without using any detergent. If you have stains on certain items, you can even use vinegar to treat them directly by pouring a little bit on and rubbing clean with a cloth.

2) Clean...lots of other stuff. You can use white vinegar to clean almost everything. It's an excellent greaseless cleaner and deodorizer for your refrigerator, sinks, garbage disposal, countertops, and floors. It can even be used to clean windows - just mix it with an equal amount of water in a spray bottle.

3) Unclog your drain. Another great use if you also have baking soda handy. First, boil a pot of water and pour it down a clogged drain. Second, pour one cup of baking soda and one cup of vinegar down the drain. Let it sit and "fizz" for five to 10 minutes. Finally, flush the drain again with another pot of boiling water. Repeat as necessary until the clog is gone.

4) Remove wrinkles. Of course, you could iron your clothes. But if you don't have the time, an iron, or just don't feel like it, add one part white vinegar to three parts water in a spray bottle. Spritz the wrinkled item lightly and hang it to dry. Even further, hang it in the bathroom while you take a shower. The steam will help release the wrinkles!

5) Kill weeds. Yes, you could pull weeds out at the root to get rid of them, and no, you probably won't desperately need vinegar for this right now. But it's still pretty cool, and knowledge of it would impress the 'rents. Come to think of it, it's hard to get to those weeds that grow out of driveway cracks...

6) Repel pests. You can use the same spray bottle you used on wrinkles (one part vinegar to three parts water) to repel ants, spiders, and other bugs. For mice, rats, and other rodents, soak some cotton balls in vinegar and place them around the house wherever you think the animals are entering - they hate the smell!

7) Clean your produce. It would help if you hung onto that spray bottle because it's great at removing bacteria from fruits and vegetables. Spray your produce, give it a light scrub, and rinse off with water.

8) Take care of your car. Well, the exterior, anyways. Use vinegar to remove bird droppings, dead bugs, bumper stickers, or decals. Use it on the windows in the winter to keep frost from forming, and use it to wipe down windshield wipers to increase their effectiveness.

9) Let's not forget about cooking.

#48: SELL YOUR STUFF

Two major concerns are inescapable for any teenager: **making money** and **cleaning**. Let's tackle both simultaneously with this one while looking entirely responsible to your overlords (aka parents).

You almost certainly have many things lying around that you don't use, need, or want. While this clutter takes up valuable space in your room, house, and life, it could also be used to generate *income*.

Consider how much money you can make by decluttering your living space. Look into various online platforms like eBay, Craigslist, and thredUP, where you can list items like furniture, electronics, clothes, and books (obviously not this one) that you no longer need but still have value. Plato's Closet is a great physical location to bring clothes, accessories, and shoes still in good condition. Selling stuff instantly frees up space for better things - and, again - MONEY.

Especially since many of these things get thrown out anyways, selling is a no-brainer. You could even make it into a little business if you're ambitious enough. Just make sure to get the OK from the overlords first. We don't want to deprive little Jimmy of his hand-me-downs.

#49: MIRROR MAGIC

We don't all have the luxury of living in ideal conditions. Whether we live with our parents, a roommate, a partner, or alone, we don't always have the means or funds to transform a house into a palace or a room into a sanctuary. One of my bedrooms growing up felt like a shoebox (it wasn't even that small, I was just a brat). Often, I felt my hangout spot wasn't "vibey" enough to invite people to.

However, there is a magical tool that can instantly upgrade your living space. There are two ways, I've found, that **mirrors** can radically do this:

Enhancing Light

You can increase the light reflecting off surfaces and into your room by hanging a few strategically-placed mirrors. Your first choice should be natural light - place a mirror across from a window or to the side of it and watch as your space brightens. If you don't have much natural light, try placing lamps on either side of a large wall mirror to reflect their glow. Mirrors can double your light, so position them to do so.

Light also creates ambiance. If this is what you're going for, positioning mirrors in places with soft lighting (such as near candles) can help create a romantic or elegant atmosphere by casting that light in multiple directions. This is great for having people over for dinner or adding style to your living space.

Enlarging a Room

Mirrors, especially tall ones, can make a room feel drastically larger by creating an illusion of extra depth. Reflecting natural light into dark corners will also make it look like a larger space.

Other great spots in the house for mirrors would be in entryways, hallways, and corridors to make those places feel huge. One of my favorite design tricks is placing a full-length mirror in the corner of two walls - another optical illusion that makes the room look more spacious.

You can also try the opposite and do some exciting things with a bunch of small round mirrors. Try clustering them together on one wall to make a one-of-a-kind art piece, and notice how the reflections play off each other and the furniture to create a unique atmosphere.

#50: THE BIG, COOL WATER BOTTLE

Allow me to introduce you to my water bottle:

It is no ordinary water bottle. This bad boy is a Boroux 16.9 oz "borosilicate glass" hydration vessel. It's almost unbreakable, BPA-free, and non-toxic. The borosilicate glass allows it to resist thermal shock - meaning you can pour boiling water into it and then cool water right after, with no problem. On top of that, it has a two-and-a-half-inch wide mouth, stainless steel lid, and a silicone, leak-proof seal.

Since you can't use mine, I suggest you find your *own* very cool water bottle. Of course, it's not about the bottle - it's about the water. You see, water is a cure-all. It's the key ingredient to life, with benefits including (but not limited to):

- natural detoxification
- better skin tone and complexion
- improved digestion and metabolism
- increased energy levels
- greater physical stamina
- joint lubrication
- weight control
- improved mood

Some people are on top of their water-consumption game. But in my case, I've realized that I naturally drink *less* water without a designated bottle.

Why a "big" bottle? Depending on our size, age, and some other factors, it's recommended that we drink anywhere from 60 to 125 ounces of water each day. Since that's so broad, don't stress over the numbers - the takeaway is that you should drink lots of water! Your big bottle will serve as a constant reminder that you should keep up your hydration. Gulp half of it before you go to bed. Wake up and chug the other half. Bring your bottle to school; keep it in your bag. The bigger it is, the less often you'll have to refill it.

Why a "cool" bottle? The fact that I like my water bottle makes me *want* to keep it by my nightstand, carry it around the house, and bring it to the gym. Face it - if you have some boring, run-of-the-mill 12-ouncer, it will eventually get left behind. But if you have one with really cool features, and it's covered with pop fidgets, unicorns, or Yoda - chances are it's in for the long haul.

If you are serious about staying on track with your water consumption and want to take it a step further, there are water bottles you can buy (or easily make with a permanent marker) that **track** how much you drink through the hours of the day.

So, get online and start browsing for a bad boy of your own.

#51: SIMPLE SWAPS

You've heard of "Eat This, Not That!" - and that's essentially what this hack is about. Eating the right things is a massive part of staying healthy, so any way you can make that easier is a win in my book (again, I definitely intended this horrible pun).

The list of swaps is virtually endless, but I'll scratch the surface and give you a few examples. Placing myself into teenage shoes again, these are some that I would be implementing - but as always, I encourage you to find ones that work for you!

SWAP...	FOR...
Soda	Sparkling water with a slice of lemon or lime
Ice cream	Frozen banana slices with peanut butter and dark chocolate chips
French fries	Oven-baked sweet potato wedges sprinkled with cinnamon sugar or sea salt and olive oil
Sugary cereal	Oatmeal topped with fresh fruit or Greek yogurt parfait made with berries and granola
Potato chips	Baked kale or zucchini chips
White rice	Brown rice or quinoa
Mayonnaise	Avocado or hummus
Milk chocolate	Dark chocolate that is at least 70% cocoa
Fruit juice	Whole fruits
Candy	Mixed raw nuts or popcorn
Sugary granola bars	Brands that use natural sweeteners like honey or maple syrup
Fried chicken	Baked or grilled chicken
Pasta	Veggie noodles or spaghetti squash

Do the healthier versions all taste as good? Well, not necessarily at first – but you can grow to love them. Practice balance, making mini-moves here and there to improve your eating habits over time. That said, I'm still a fan of letting the occasional Reese's Cup slip through the cracks.

#52: WORK IN WEIGHTS

Honestly, this is a trick I use all the time now - but I wish I had started younger. It all began a few years ago when a friend and I challenged each other to lose some weight.

The goal was to lose ten pounds in two months while not starving ourselves and still eating healthy. I had a solid workout routine and knew I could cut a few calories here and there to make it happen. And I did - we both did. What shocked me was HOW my friend did it. Ready for this?

His daily routine didn't change. He ate the same way and didn't implement any workout regimen. He did *exactly* all the same things he had before the challenge. The difference? He strapped three-pound ankle weights on as often as possible - sometimes even wrist weights. **GENIUS.**

Granted, my friend walked a mile and a half to work every morning, so the added weight really paid off there. But think about it: by doing this, you're basically turning yourself into a **superhero**, enhancing every action and multiplying its effectiveness! Going up and down stairs, taking hikes, walking the dog, blow-drying your hair, brushing your teeth, doing chores - heck, if you're skilled enough, there's got to be a way to even pull this off at school on certain days.

No, you can't always be in a situation where you have weights strapped to you - especially in the summer wearing shorts. Not a good look. But they DO make them sleek now (unlike in the 80s), to the point where pants could potentially cover them up. They are also adjustable, so you can start light and increase weight when needed.

Whether your goal is to shed a few pounds, tone, or increase strength and speed, this will do it ALL without you having to do anything else but live your life! I still don't know where my friend came up with this idea, but I'm glad he did.

I should wear finger weights while writing my books.

#53: OUTSMART OVEREATING

Your health will *always* be your true wealth, even though you might only appreciate that once you're older. It's best to start being conscious of this before it smacks you in the face later on, and eating the **right amount** is one way to do that.

Overeating can occur for many reasons. Sometimes we eat out of boredom. Other times, we may eat to deal with stress. Many of us overeat when we aren't even hungry as a form of escapism or to reward ourselves. We fill the void in our lives with food rather than confronting our problems.

As always, I'm going to be honest with you: I'm a foodie. The struggle for self-control is real when faced with a deep-dish pizza or a pile of hot dogs. In some ways, the challenge of not overeating is the bane of my existence! But I have found a few techniques that help me outsmart this struggle. And yes, I will share them with you.

1) Eat before you eat. If you're afraid you might overeat at breakfast, lunch, or dinner, consider consuming something light 15-20 minutes before the meal. A few raw veggies, a small apple, a handful of nuts, yogurt, or even chugging a bunch of water. Your stomach will be unable to hold as much food when it comes down to it, and naturally, your appetite will be suppressed.

2) Eat your meals on a smaller plate. Sound silly? Well, it helps to a degree. Plate size can trick the mind when it comes to eating. Yes, there's a tendency to put more food on a larger dish - so you're grabbing less on the practical side. But also, on the psychological side, a fuller small plate lends the *illusion* that you are consuming more than you actually are.

3) Grocery shop on a full stomach. Your parents may do the grocery shopping for the house, but hey - it's time for you to start getting involved in that, anyways! When my stomach starts growling and I enter a place of food, I become a kid in a candy store. EVERYTHING goes into the cart. The problem is that I stock the house with lots of guilty pleasure food (while tripling the price). Shopping after I've eaten always makes the grocery trip much more realistic.

4) Never take the whole bag/container with you. If you're leaving the kitchen or closet with a snack, make sure NOT to take the entire package of chips, popcorn, chocolates, or anything else in bulk. Break it down into a small bowl or mug. If it's in front of you, you'll eat it (again, I'm talking to myself here). Get in the habit of controlling portions before temptation can set in.

5) Eat more fiber. This is one of my favorite methods of keeping the calorie count down. Fibrous foods like nuts, seeds, fruits, and vegetables will fill you up faster and are generally lower in calories (nuts are the exception). They will also satiate you for a more extended period. I go for fruit and raw veggies because my body can run through the motion of "snacking" for longer without the guilt.

6) Chew more slowly. If you can do this, more power to you. I cannot.

HIDDEN HACK: HELP OTHERS WHENEVER YOU CAN (THIS IS WHERE I NEED YOU!)

"If you light a lamp for somebody, it will also brighten your path."

— BUDDHA

Why?

Well, partly because it's just a thing good humans do - but there are plenty of ways it elevates your game, too:

- Helping other people makes *you* feel good (there's actually science behind this)
- It enables you to be part of a community
- You strengthen your sense of purpose
- It increases your self-esteem
- You become a leader by example

Helping others can come in many forms. On a large scale, it might be voluntary work for a homeless shelter or care home. On a small scale, it might be lending someone money or helping them with a personal problem. And while you're here racking up the hacks to make adulthood a breeze, it could be the act of helping someone *else* acquire those hacks.

The great news is that you can do that **now** with barely any effort.

By leaving a review of this book on Amazon and telling new readers how it's helped *you*, you'll lead them to *their* benefits. Your review will also help ME greatly by allowing me to continue writing these semi-witty but highly-empowering books!

So, *thank you in advance for being so supportive*. Your quick review is a gift I'll carry my entire life.

Scan the QR Code below to leave a review!

5

MONEY

"Money is a terrible master but an excellent servant."

— P.T. BARNUM

It doesn't matter what form currency takes - gold, silver, copper, nickel, printed paper, credit, crypto, or even the barter system. The physical representation of money has changed over time, and it will change again. Regardless of its form, know that real wealth comes from an *exchange of value*.

My goal for this chapter is to give you "macro" hacks to navigate wealth development, more so than the fine-tuned aspects of money management.

The reason for this? Well, if you embody wealth at a macro level, it won't matter what form money takes - you'll know how to make it work for you, how to create more of it, and how to multiply it exponentially. We live in crazy times and can't assume that today's systems will be the same in five years, one year, or even tomorrow! Better to *teach* you how to fish than to *give* you a few fish (ask your parents). Although I'll also provide tangible "micro" hacks, I've set the big picture on helping you understand **what money is**. I'd also like to push the boundaries of what money *means* to you. We obviously need money to survive and thrive - but does more money make us happy, or does being happy make us more money?

Unlike the "chicken or the egg" scenario, the "money or happiness" scenario DOES have a definitive answer. And I'm not regurgitating the old cliché "money can't buy happiness," either (although it is true). There is more to this, and I want to give you the plain and simple **truth**. Because as far as I know, they aren't teaching it in school.

So before diving into the chapter, please sit with and try to absorb this one massive truth bomb: **money only amplifies what's already inside you.**

Think of money as gasoline to your fire. If a miserable, poor person received a ton of money, they would *still be miserable* after obtaining it (once the immediate sense of joy wore off). In fact, they would more than likely become MORE miserable. And that's because their **mindset**, which caused them to be poor and miserable in the first place, wouldn't have been fundamentally changed. Metaphorically, adding "gasoline" to a mentality of lack, control, or jealousy will cause wildfire and destruction. Don't take my word for it - do your research! Learn how time and time again, a lottery winner previously in poverty has inevitably gone bankrupt (or worse) after receiving a large sum of money. Or more commonly, how some of the wealthiest people in the world can also be the most depressed. It is undoubtedly a false belief that "more money" will bring you the satisfaction you desire.

Conversely, when a person cultivates an abundant mindset and a correct knowledge of wealth, money will only amplify that happiness - a controlled, effective fire that creates warmth, light, and even more opportunity.

Back to our cause and effect, the chicken or the egg. Money may not bring true happiness, but happiness doesn't automatically make you rich, either. So, what truly comes before the money? Well, the answer to that is: *the energy*.

HACK #54: VIEW MONEY AS ENERGY

"The secret to wealth is simple: Find a way to do more for others than anyone else does. Become more valuable. Do more. Give more. Be more. Serve more."

— TONY ROBBINS

Yes, money is simply energy. It's a medium of exchange *representing* your value to the outside world. Broken down to its core, this means two things to me: 1) If you want more money, give more value. And 2) Your financial success mirrors your personal energy (as "like attracts like"). Let's tackle the first one first.

If you want more money, give more value.

How do you give more value and increase your intrinsic wealth? I don't expect you to know all that yet - lord knows I didn't. But this IS something you should keep in mind moving forward. First, consider what you're good at and what kind of services or products you could provide to others. I believe that every single person has something incredibly unique to offer. Start becoming aware of ways to create income streams around your uniqueness. Whether it's developing a trade, craft, tutoring, entertaining, selling services or products, or starting your own business - the goal should be prioritizing *value* over *money*. I will explore this further in the "Job & Career" section. For now, I just want you to understand it.

Your financial success mirrors your personal energy.

In my opinion, you've got to internalize this "money mindset" before you start applying techniques. Remember: your energy is the *cause*; money is the *effect*. If you *think* you're poor, you are. If you think in lack, you will be lacking. Know that you deserve it, and it will come to you. Hoard it, and it will bite you. If you want to receive more, you must give more. Wealth is not tangible; none of us *actually* care about money - we want the freedom, lifestyle, and expansion it brings us. Learn to live in the energy field of that abundance first, and I PROMISE money will follow. As Tony states above: **BE more**. If you knew that your outside world reflected your inside world, who would you **be** on the inside?

#55: MASTER BASIC FINANCIAL LITERACY

Now that you're walking the walk, you can start talking the talk. You don't need a degree in finance or economics – right now, the goal of financial literacy should be to *establish a basic understanding of a broad number of terms*. This will majorly empower you and set you up for the future. I've organized the basic terms you need to get started - something no one did for me when I was your age!

Money 101:

1) **Balance** - The total amount of money in your bank or other financial accounts.

2) **Income** - Money you earn from a job or other activity, typically reported on tax returns.

3) **Expenses** - The cost of goods or services, including rent, utilities, food, insurance, and taxes.

4) **Budget** - An organized plan for how you will use your money each month; often includes income and expenses so that you can track where your money is going and make wise decisions about spending it in the future.

5) **Checking** - A type of bank account that allows you to withdraw money and make payments.

6) **Savings** - A type of bank account where you deposit money to save and earn interest over time.

7) **Interest** - The amount of money you earn on your savings account or other investments or a fee paid for borrowing money over time from a lender or bank (calculated as a percentage of the amount borrowed).

8) **Loan** - Generally, an agreement between the borrower (you) and the lender (bank or other financial institution) to lend a specified amount of money in exchange for repayment with interest.

9) Credit Card - A type of credit (loan). It can be used to purchase goods and services, with the expectation that you will pay off the balance each month.

10) Debt - Money you owe to someone else, usually with interest included.

11) Assets - Anything that has value; something you own with monetary worth. Examples include cash, investments, savings, real estate, and jewelry.

12) Liabilities - Debts owed by you; the opposite of assets (an example is student loans).

13) Investment - Putting money into something with the expectation of gaining benefit from it over time (this could be stocks, real estate, a business, or anything else with growth potential).

14) Taxes - A percentage of money you must pay the government based on your earnings or other financial activity.

15) Credit Score - A numerical representation of your credit "worthiness." This is determined by looking at factors like payment history and debt usage.

16) Stock - A share of ownership in a company. When you purchase stock, you are investing in the company and buying a portion of it.

17) Gross - The total amount of money you make before subtracting taxes and other financial obligations.

18) Net - The amount of money you have left after subtracting taxes and financial obligations.

#56: "CASH IN" ON BEFRIENDING YOUR PARENTS

I can't stress enough here that in NO way am I suggesting you "use" your parents for monetary gain or use them (or anyone else) in ANY unethical way in the least.

Instead, I want to open your eyes to yet another tremendous benefit of developing a good relationship with your parents (or any other adult who may play a parental role in your life). And I've placed this piece of advice right here because it should come *specifically* before the next two.

Even if your parents aren't necessarily wealthy or well-off, I can guarantee they know more about money than you do. Why? Because our parents, and elders in general, have had more time on this planet to build up a certain level of knowledge and experience when it comes to money matters.

Learning money is like learning a language - in some ways, it *is* a language. The person speaking that language for longer naturally knows more expressions, colloquialisms, and idioms than you could ever learn in your brief study period.

The great part is that once you have a solid relationship with your parents, all you have to do is **ask** for their help. In case you have yet to notice, parents *love* to give advice. Trust me - you want the money advice! So, when the time is right, ask your parents for the single best piece of money advice they can offer you, and then let the floodgates open.

Other things you should start picking their brains on:

- setting up your bank account(s)
- budgeting
- compensating you for chores
- getting a part-time job
- negotiating for better prices
- worthwhile investments
- potentially matching what you put away for savings

Unfortunately, many families believe that discussing money is private or taboo. This is why *so many* young adults are completely uninformed about it once it comes time to move out! Make it clear that your interest is solely in **learning about and being responsible with your money**, not prying into theirs.

You might be surprised at how much your parents are willing to share and assist you with. And, if nothing else, having more open-minded conversations about money *now* will prepare you for more open-minded discussions in the *future*. That level of preparedness is invaluable!

#57: SET UP YOUR ACCOUNTS ASAP

I know, I just told you to ask your parents how to do this. But this book can be used in tandem with their advice. I'm very aware that many young people don't have good home lives and that getting help from parents isn't an option. So, I'd like to set some framework regardless. Also, utilizing multiple perspectives will set you up to make the best decisions.

When it comes to setting up your first bank account, it's a relatively simple process. If you're under 18, you'll likely need your parents to **co-sign** the application - but it should still be in your name. All monthly statements should come to you. Your parents will act as "training wheels" to get you going.

Assuming they're on board and you're doing this together, the first step is researching banks and their features. Aim to make choices that benefit both your short and long-term needs. Some things to look for in "features" are:

- Fee structure and monthly costs
- Online vs. branch access (or a combination of both)
- Access to ATMs and branches in other cities
- Interest rates on savings accounts or checking accounts
- Overdraft protection options (such as linkages to other accounts)

After deciding on a bank, you can complete an **application** online or in person. You'll need identification (driver's license, birth certificate, etc.) and proof of address. You may also be required to provide a certain amount of money to open the account; this varies by bank (hence the importance of doing your research).

I recommend opening one **checking** and one **savings** account to begin. Your checking account will be primarily used for day-to-day expenses (food, spending money, paying bills, etc.). Your savings account is where you'll store money over time for more significant expenses (a laptop, vehicle, college tuition - you get the idea). Because both accounts are held at the same bank, they will almost certainly be linked, making it easier to transfer funds between them as needed.

And then, you'll get your first **ATM (debit) card**. That's a very cool feeling! Now you'll be able to access your money anytime, anywhere. And this is only the beginning when it comes to managing your finances. Just remember that with this new power comes *responsibility*. And nothing teaches responsibility like overdraft charges on your brand-new bank account.

#58: BUDGET ASAP

Your budget serves as the foundation of your financial structure. A budget gives you the **clarity** you need to take control of your finances. Conversely, you are gambling with your money if you don't have one in place. It's like playing darts with your eyes closed - your chances of success are slim.

Budgeting aims to *categorize your expenses so you can effectively see where your money is going.* This will help you make better financial decisions, stay organized, and achieve goals more quickly. But it doesn't have to be overcomplicated. We could go down the rabbit hole on budgeting techniques, but there's no need to bite off more than you can chew at this stage.

First, determine where you are: how many, if any, expenses do you have? How much income do you have, and how steady is it? Do you particularly enjoy the thought of budgeting? Do you like working with numbers and money?

The last two questions may seem inconsequential, but they're actually very relevant. As you progress through this money journey, you'll see that success requires a certain level of discipline and attitude. So, if you already know that numbers aren't your thing, take caution not to make the process more nuanced than it needs to be. I'll provide three simple strategies to get you started:

1) (Very) Basic Budgeting. The return of the 80/20 rule! And it doesn't get simpler than this: **put aside 20% of everything you make**. I suggest starting here if you don't have any actual expenses or if your income is small and inconsistent. Doing this will put you in the habit of saving and inspire you as you watch your savings grow. Of course, you can tweak the percentage, but I like one-fifth because it's so simple and effective - you don't even need a calculator!

2) Intermediate Level Budgeting. If you're at the stage where you've got regular income and are responsible for some expenses, try the popular **50/30/20 budgeting rule**. Don't let the numbers scare you - it's still pretty basic. In this model, 50% of your income should go to necessities (like food and bills), 30% can be allocated for wants (such as clothing and entertainment), and 20% should be reserved for savings. Again, the ratio can be adjusted depending on how many expenses you're responsible for (but I don't recommend going below 20% on savings).

3) (Slightly) Advanced Budgeting. You should calculate a **detailed budget** if you've got a part-time job, expenses, and a desire to fine-tune. To do this, it would be best to map out ALL your expenses and income streams. This can be done on paper or with one of the many budgeting apps. You can determine your budget *weekly* or *monthly* - decide which works best for your schedule. Check out this weekly budget as an example:

Weekly Budget

NAME: Derek **DATE:** 3/5 - 3/11

My Income

DATE	DESCRIPTION	AMOUNT
3/7	Sold game	$15
3/10	Paycheck	$110
3/11	Allowance	$25

My Expenses

DATE	DESCRIPTION	AMOUNT
3/10	Phone	$10
3/8	Gas	$30
-	Food/Snacks	$25

Notes

20% of $150 into Savings = $30

$85 - 30 = $55 spending money!

(I should start a separate savings for a cat...)

TOTAL EXPENSE: $65

TOTAL INCOME: $150

TOTAL REMAINING: $85

****Keep in mind that by "income," I'm referring to "net" income - the money you're left with **after** taxes.****

#59: DON'T SAY I NEVER GAVE YOU ANYTHING

All this talk about bank accounts, budgeting, and income - but how *do* you make money as a teenager? School will consume most of your week, homework is an extension of that, and a well-deserved break is needed on the weekends, right? I don't believe you should break your back working while in high school. However, I think it's wise to start generating *some* income right now – it will teach you responsibility, give you more freedom, and allow you to start saving early on.

And so, I've created this lovely little list for you. Some of these might be obvious, and some might seem obscure. But either way, I hope they get your creative juices flowing and lead you to new money-making possibilities – while still leaving time for *fun*.

30 Income Ideas

Part-Time/Seasonal

1. Food industry/customer service (restaurant, coffee shop, etc.)
2. Movie theater, grocery store, or mall
3. Drive for a delivery service (Grubhub, Doordash, etc.)
4. Train to be a lifeguard
5. Camp counselor
6. Receptionist at gym, health center, salon, etc.
7. Work at an amusement park
8. Event catering

All Online

9. Sell handmade items/jewelry
10. Start a blog or podcast
11. Sell clothes on sites like Etsy, Poshmark, or Facebook Marketplace
12. Create tutorial videos on YouTube
13. Graphic design
14. Get paid for online surveys like Survey Junkie or Swagbucks
15. Referral or commission program

Entrepreneur/Crafty

16. Teach a skill you know (music, sport, coding, etc.)
17. DJ parties or events
18. Personal assistant
19. Collect and recycle cans and bottles
20. Sell your art at fairs, craft shows, or flea markets
21. Affiliate marketing

Community/Neighborhood

22. Babysitting
23. Pet-sitting/dog walking
24. Chores/housework
25. Mowing lawns/landscape work
26. Tutor younger students in a skill or subject
27. Snow removal/shoveling
28. House-sitting and cleaning
29. Wash/detail cars
30. Window cleaning

#60: PAY IT FORWARD

You've got some cash and your new debit card - you're feeling good. Now, we want to transform that good feeling into a *flow* – to activate the ocean of wealth and abundance that is YOU.

The act of "paying it forward" is a straight-up game-changer, in my opinion. And this is the standard definition: "When someone does something for you, instead of paying them back directly, you pass it on to someone else." But I view it more straightforward: **do something nice for someone else, expecting nothing in return**. It may seem strange at the outset to tell you that giving money away is a "money hack." Well, please wait before returning this book! If you know me by now, you know I'm not here to push garbage - so let's look deeper...

Primarily, remember again that **money is energy**. Abundance flows; it's not stagnant. Therefore, it needs to move to *and* from you. When you give more and do it genuinely (key!), you directly signal to your subconscious mind that you *have* money to share - that you are **already wealthy**. And as with everything else, once your subconscious truly believes something, it is a DONE DEAL. Simply put, start telling the story of *"I am wealthy"* rather than the tired tale of *"I'm so broke."*

A regular way that I consistently practice this is in tipping. I always try to be extra generous, especially if the service or experience has been personable. And it always feels good, as I'm sure it does for the recipient. It's like a secret little handshake I have with the Universe that says, "Hey! I'm grateful for what I have - let's expand on this. Here you go!" It doesn't matter if you have a little or a lot of money - **it's about the intention behind the action, not the dollar amount**. Why wait for Christmas, or one day a year, to give? What a waste. Make it Christmas every day!

I can't exactly prove how giving more out of the kindness of your heart will turn into more money for you. But if you want to do it for that reason, you've already missed the point. Think about the notion of karma, the boomerang effect, "what goes around comes around." I've lived this and see it every day and all around me, so you'll have to have a little faith here.

PS - Why do you think the wealthiest people donate a portion of their money to charities and other good causes (besides the tax write-off)? It's because they understand that true wealth can't live in a vacuum - meaning, it has to be shared and circulated. And just as the wealthy give, they, in turn, become wealthier. Why not grasp this at a young age, and start putting it into practice now?

#61: FORGET ABOUT DEBIT

I know - that debit card is fantastic. It's shiny. You can swipe it, and you *get* stuff. It even has your name on it! And you can use it to pick some door locks (note: don't do this illegally). Well, don't worry - we're not abandoning the card altogether.

But it may be wise to **use it just once at the beginning of each week**.

Sorry, but until you've advanced in money management, it's best to avoid using a debit card as much as possible. It's just way too easy to overspend. Even though a debit card functions like cash, swiping that thing around *feels* different. Your brain doesn't perceive the funds vanishing from your bank account as if you were handing over physical money. There's something about paying with cash that makes us think twice about what we're buying - in a good way!

That's why, for now, I suggest using the card to withdraw *only* your weekly budgeted cash. You'll be able to see and feel exactly how much money you've spent and how much you still have left. Remember that your money is there to serve you, not be your master. Therefore, you must demonstrate discipline before wielding that little plastic sword.

Don't worry. Your card still knows you love it. You'll get more bonding time soon enough.

#62: GET IT ON CREDIT

Like the debit card, a credit card is a double-edged sword. The difference here is, well – the ability to build credit. And, like it or not, your credit score (or "creditworthiness") is necessary in this current world.

The downside of having a credit card, especially at a young age, is the temptation to spend money you don't have. This can be a huge financial pitfall and create long-term debt issues. As I mentioned, the upside is that it allows you to build up your **credit score**. This boosts your ability to take out loans, get mortgages, buy cars, and increase the amount of money you can ultimately borrow (and the interest rate at which you can borrow it). And we're going to do that strategically.

For our purposes right now, there's no need to go too deeply into credit score numbers (as a general rule at the time of writing this, try and keep it above 700). I just want you to 1) have a basic understanding of the principle and 2) show you how to start building that score up *now*.

Step 1) Start by getting a low-limit credit card, preferably issued by your bank. *Something to keep in mind:* you must be at least 18 years old to sign up for a credit card, and even that can be tricky under the age of 21. But it is doable, especially if you can prove a steady income. That said, if your parents (with whom you now have a great relationship with *cough cough*) agree, you can be an **authorized user** in most cases. When this happens, late or missed payments will harm *both* parties - so that's extra responsibility on YOU (hey, I never said this part was easy).

Step 2) Use the card responsibly and keep track of all your payments and spending - don't go overboard. Set a fixed amount you will use each month, and stick to it strictly. Somewhere between 10% to 30% of your credit limit is a great target (for instance, if your credit limit is $300, keep your spending around $30 to $90 per month). This small step starts building your **credit history**.

Step 3) Pay off the *entire* balance each month and **on time**. This is paramount – it's the biggest factor in your credit score! Late payments will likewise hurt your score and, as previously stated, can take a long time to recover from.

Of course, other factors will affect your credit score, too (consistent employment, length of credit history, etc.) - but this is no doubt a great place to start.

#63: SEEK DELAYED GRATIFICATION (PART 1)

"Achievers don't submit to instant gratification; they INVEST in the LONG-TERM payoff."

— DARREN HARDY

There's no denying that we live in a world of instant gratification. It's everywhere – we can have food delivered to our doorstep instantly, buy anything online and have it arrive the next day, or get the latest technology in just a few clicks. And because this is how we are taught to "survive" in today's society, our brains are wired to want everything **now**.

The "marshmallow experiment" (conducted by psychology professor Walter Mischel in the 1970s) is a well-known study that makes this point glaringly obvious. He presented a group of children with a marshmallow and offered them a simple choice: eat the treat immediately, or wait 15 minutes and receive *two*.

Some children chose to wait for the second marshmallow, while others succumbed to their desire for **instant gratification** and ate the one they were given. But the experiment's further studies were eye-opening: the children who *waited* became more successful later in life. Those who **delayed gratification** were better able to control themselves and more likely to succeed in the long run.

It turns out it's not just marshmallows. The ability to delay gratification has been linked with other positive outcomes, including higher SAT scores, better social skills, lower levels of substance abuse, and healthier overall lifestyles.

I want you to pay close attention to this sentence: As a teen, you have ONE significant advantage over every adult - **TIME**. And although I will expand on this later, it has enormous implications for our current conversation about money.

As an example, consider compound interest. In this structure, the interest you earn on money is amplified (compounded) upon itself rather than added to your original (principal) amount. This makes a big difference over time. Suppose you start investing when you're young and leave it compounding over years and decades. In that case, compounding can exponentially multiply your investments more than someone who starts later in life - even if their investments are the same.

Assume you put $1,000 in a 5% interest account and leave it alone. That's a relatively small amount, but you'd have earned $50 in interest by the end of a year. If you leave the same money in the account for another year, you'll have made over $100; if you leave it alone for three years, your total earnings will be around $160. All from simply leaving your money alone and letting compound interest do its thing. Now imagine if you continued to contribute to this fund regularly!

Time will also benefit your money by creating a larger emergency fund, a bigger nest egg for your 20s, and larger returns in stocks or investments (if you choose that route). Let that sink in, and get curious about ways time and money can *work for you.*

Getting into the habit of saving is essential - it's a big part of mastering money. But ultimately, cultivating the **quality** of delayed gratification within yourself will become one of your greatest assets.

6

SPIRIT/ATTITUDE

"Yesterday I was clever, so I wanted to change the world. Today I am wise, so I am changing myself."

— RUMI

Welcome to my favorite part of the book.

Within the other sections, I've certainly done my homework to find you helpful advice on various life topics. After all, I want you to succeed in *all* ways - and to do that, you need tried and true tactics. But in this section, I want to go beyond that to talk about one of the most important aspects of life that *doesn't* come from research: **wisdom**.

Wisdom is *embodied knowledge*. You can know everything there is to know, but if you can't internalize, reflect, and apply it to your life meaningfully, then none of that knowledge matters, does it?

What I'm about to give you are "wisdom shortcuts." **Mind hacks**. These are seeds that, if you choose to water now, will result in magnificent growth throughout your entire life - and change everything you think you know about existence. I will, admittedly, take a little more liberty in offering what I feel is truly valuable here. This section is not meticulously garnered from books, articles, or the internet (directly, anyway). I've been compiling this inspiration for the past year or so, and this is my attempt at consolidating and packaging it in easy-to-grasp ways for you.

Do not skip this chapter! Read on with an open mind - that is the only way the knowledge will work for *YOU*. That being said, there is a lot to chew on here. If a section doesn't click with you yet, move on to what does – you can always return later. But I promise you, at some point, it will *all* come together. We only evolve by "standing on the shoulders of giants"; by learning from those who have gone before us. I encourage you to leapfrog my experience and knowledge to reach your own revelations faster!

Remember this: your mindset, spirit, and attitude will ultimately define you and your life. Knowledge of your*self* will open up doors for you. And the application of this knowledge, combined with discipline, is the only path to true wisdom.

HACK #64: ENJOY (IN-JOY)

We're going to take a little journey. So, let's start here - *in the moment.*

As it turns out, this moment is all you (or any of us) will ever be. We won't get too deep yet, however. For obvious reasons, I'm going to assume you're a teenager. Understand that adolescence is such a short phase – roughly 8% of your total life experience. If a human body pictured the span of your life, the teen years would basically equate to *one forearm.* Not even a whole arm! Regardless of how it may feel, it will pass by very, very quickly.

But adolescence is also a magical time - a brief window in which you virtually live for free, develop exponentially, and arguably experience the most exciting moments you'll ever experience. Consider how many adults have said, *"If I could have that time back..." "If I knew then what I know now..." "If I could only do it again..."*

Unfortunately, you can't go back and do it again - but you *can* live in the moment. You *can* appreciate everything that's right in front of you. And you can **enjoy it**.

I know there is so much going on. I was a teenager, too. I also know the deep yearning to be an adult - to live independently, make your own decisions, drink legally, be respected...heck, to sit at the "grown-up" table at family gatherings. Time flies in the whirlwind of school, dating, friends, family, and self-discovery - and time drags in the monotony of homework, tests, chores, and the desire to grow up. So where does that leave you?

It leaves you in the moment - where you will always be. So do your work. Take your tests. Go on awkward dates. Finish your chores. Make your mistakes. Face your challenges. But do your BEST not to lose yourself in it all. Strive to maintain a broader perspective, knowing this is a short, precious time. And most importantly, do as much of it as you possibly can **in joy** - the highest frequency of life we have.

#65: THE PATH OF LEAST RESISTANCE

What it's not: Taking the easy way out. Backing down from what you believe in. Not standing up for yourself. Being lazy. Giving up.

What it is: Moving in the direction of your natural inclination. Following the path that feels right to you. Listening to your gut instead of your "idea" of what needs to be done.

I must be clear about this so you don't misinterpret it - I'm coming from a place of spirit and soul essence here, not a literal or physical one.

To follow the "path of least resistance" is to live eloquently, gracefully, and powerfully - yet somehow, we've been screwing it up for ages. It comes down to developing your intuition, then going with the flow of life using your natural skills, heart, and passion to succeed effortlessly. So many words for such a simple concept!

Let's break it down to just one word: **water**.

"Be like water making its way through cracks. Do not be assertive, but adjust to the object, and you shall find a way around or through it. If nothing within you stays rigid, outward things will disclose themselves...Be water, my friend."

— BRUCE LEE

Water is the perfect metaphor for this idea: no matter *what* path water takes, it will always be the simplest, gentlest, and least obstructive way from point A to point B. Water does not fight to go upstream. It doesn't argue or struggle - it yields. It doesn't waste any energy trying to take a difficult route - it just flows to its destination. And that's what our lives should look like.

We should be in a "flow state" as often as possible - doing what comes naturally and easily without feeling resistance or struggle. And it's so much easier than you think! The more you practice, the easier it will be to find your groove. But it's important to discern between "laziness" and the path of least resistance - one will keep you stuck, while the other can lead to greatness. Inertia and forward momentum are still involved, but it's done in *alignment with who you are.*

I will give you a basic example in the form of a true story:

When I was in fifth grade, I was sort of a nerd. And some friends in my group were *very* good at math. Seeing them easily solve complicated problems was so remarkable and inspiring. A couple of them even entered competitions and won awards. I wanted to be at that level. I wanted those trophies and that recognition, too. And I'll be honest - I was also a bit jealous. I studied like crazy to be one of the elites, proverbially banging my head against the wall every day trying to solve that problem (hehe). It just wasn't in my DNA - good at math, I was not. But I *was* an excellent speller.

Spelling was something that came naturally to me at a very young age. And at some point, that must have clicked - because instead of continuing to struggle with math, I decided to take the path of least resistance and focus on what I was *already* good at. Although it felt lonely, I decided to enter the school spelling bee. And guess what? **I won.**

Not only did I win the school competition, but I went on to win the town and then climbed to the top of the statewide spelling bee (ultimately losing on the word "perforated" because I thought I heard "purporated" - what does that even mean?! I *knew* how to spell "perforated"! Anyways...). It turns out I was already elite, just too busy following someone else's path to see it.

So, as soon as I stopped trying to jam a square peg into a round hole, the river of life took me where I was meant to go. I experienced the joy of flowing *with* life - instead of against it.

Many martial artists use this energy preservation to turn their opponent's force against them. Many athletes use it to make their movements more powerful and efficient. I've used it throughout my life to guide me to my next level. And now you will use it to

_____.

#66: PAY (WITH) ATTENTION (PART 1)

I could write a whole book on this topic alone. And I might. Because there is just no way to stress it enough: *our attention is our most precious commodity.* And the things you choose to place your attention on are the things that will flourish in your life, quite literally - this has implications both scientifically and metaphysically.

Yes, your attention is your *true* currency. Step back and take a look at your life: what are you "paying" attention to daily? You will soon notice that the stuff you focus on regularly is the same stuff that makes up the hodgepodge of reality all around you - **the world as you know it**. Your concerns, worries, desires, and interests manifest because you pay them attention. What you focus on also determines who you are, how you think, what you do, and how you feel.

Still don't believe me that **attention** is our most valuable resource? Think about it - what's the ONE thing every website, media outlet, commercial, and advertisement *constantly* vies for? What do your parents and teachers demand of you? What about your friends, your girlfriend, your boyfriend, and even your *enemies*? That's right: YOUR ATTENTION. From now on, start imagining literal money spent every time you "pay" something with attention: view your seconds as **cents** and your minutes as **dollars**. Because that's exactly what's happening - you're investing in things. Are you spending your money wisely?

Let's look at this from the eyes of science. Physics proves that by simply observing an object or system, we can profoundly affect it - that the thing being observed fundamentally *changes*. In quantum mechanics, they call this the "observer effect." Further, when attempting to break matter down to its tiniest components (the goal of quantum physics), physicists have concluded that matter, at its core, is just slowed-down **energy** (Borowski 2012). Every single possibility is available in the quantum field. In fact, it *already exists* in a state of potential - you just have to choose it. Life is, quite literally, what you make it! (Cho 2017). If everything is essentially energy, what does that mean for this concept of attention? I believe that our attention has an *altering effect on reality itself*.

Take a minute to consider how powerful this concept is. Wherever you place your attention, that's where the energy goes. You are "choosing" possibilities from the infinite realm of the quantum field *all the time* - essentially watering seeds in a magical garden. Because so many are still unaware of this, they quickly get swept up in the daily grind, allowing external forces to pull their attention here and there without realizing how much influence and control they actually have. The world is full of greed, competition, and scarcity for many people. For others, freedom, abundance, compassion, and unity. The difference between the two is what they **consistently choose to focus on.**

It's important to note that I'm not suggesting you pretend the things you don't want *don't exist*. I'm suggesting you don't **pay** for them if they're misaligned with your desired life experience. We don't become delusional and start living in La La Land - instead, we strive to approach things from a higher point of awareness and become *deliberate* with our creative power.

Imagine being at a buffet with all the food you could possibly imagine. If you don't like asparagus, do you find yourself repeating, "*The asparagus doesn't exist...it's not real...this is not happening...the asparagus doesn't exist...*" Of course not. You just choose not to put it on your plate. To go a step further, there is no need to judge the asparagus. You acknowledge that it's an option, that some people are here for it, and you peacefully move on. The same goes for a trip to the mall - you find all the clothes you could ever want there. Wouldn't you stick to the items that fit your needs and tastes, understanding that although some might love tie-dye shirts and sequin pants, it's just a "no" from you?

Life IS a buffet table of...well, anything and everything you could ever imagine. Want distress? It's there for you - turn on the news and pay it some attention. Want unconditional love? Seek and appreciate it in yourself and your loved ones, then watch it manifest.

The good news about all of this? **You are 100% in control.**

#67: BELIEVE IN BELIEF

Do you know my response when someone asks me what I believe in? It's certainly different from what it used to be. This question overwhelmed me because I feared being "wrong," judged, or in over my head. It's a hairy subject, for sure. And as you read this, know that I don't intend to ruffle any feathers - not in the least. It's not my desire to "push" any one belief on you or to degrade another. Because these days, my response to this question is always: "I believe in *belief*."

You see, I've come not to learn but to **know** - that BELIEF holds the power, not the thing believed in. Faith (belief in the unseen) itself IS the thing that moves mountains, that paves the way for miracles.

After all, don't most religions promote and demand a certain level of belief? A dedication to something greater than the concrete, physical realm? This faith in something beyond our immediate awareness allows us to access a highly curious intelligence and power.

Yes, miracles occur because of unwavering **faith**. And you don't have to be in a designated place of worship to access divinity - that's a backward notion that's gone on far too long. Further, no beliefs are false - they are simply **self-fulfilling**. That means that whatever belief you choose to hold in your heart and act upon will be the one that expresses its truth in your life. This is not to downplay religion, science, spirituality, creeds, or dogma (the acceptable "version" of a teaching) - I'm not targeting *any* of these things. I'm talking about something much deeper: the **whole** of belief is more fundamental and sacred than any of its **parts**.

Each of us is born with this largely untapped connection to higher power, and the bridge is none other than our *subconscious mind*. It sits right below the ego, or "conscious" mind - below the ramblings of our thoughts, in a place of stillness and peace. Here, we can access our higher power - the power that "moves mountains" and performs miracles. And it's *faith* that allows us to tap into this resource like a wellspring.

This is not the time to go down the rabbit hole of the subconscious - but if you'd like to dig deeper into the mysteries of the mind, I'll suggest a few of my favorite books (you might want to wait until your 20s to tackle these):

- "The Power of Your Subconscious Mind" by Dr. Joseph Murphy
- "You Are the Placebo" by Dr. Joe Dispenza
- "The Biology of Belief" by Bruce H. Lipton, PhD
- "The Power of Intention" by Wayne W. Dyer
- "Psycho-Cybernetics" by Maxwell Maltz, M.D.
- "Feeling Is the Secret" by Neville Goddard
- "Three Magic Words" by U.S. Andersen

Now, *what* you believe in is up to you - it's your free choice as a human being. If you believe in a god or deity, this knowledge can strengthen that. If you don't or are indifferent - what do you believe about *yourself*? About others? What do you believe about the world? About your future? Your everyday assumptions about life are beliefs, too! And they shape your world just as much. The power of belief allows for ALL types of growth and cannot be denied. Because when we believe, we open ourselves up to **possibility**. What does that look like in your life?

"Because of your belief in external things, you think power into them by transferring the power that you are to the external thing. Realize you yourself are the power you have mistakenly given to outer conditions."

— NEVILLE GODDARD, "YOUR FAITH IS YOUR FORTUNE"

#68: HOLD ON LOOSELY

There was a band called "38 Special" that released a song the year I was born (you're going to have to work for that info) called "Hold On Loosely." The chorus says, "Hold on loosely, but don't let go. If you cling too tightly, you're gonna lose control." And that, right there, is the lesson - finding the balance between "letting go" and "controlling" a situation. *The art of avoiding extremes,* you could say. Let's keep this simple and break the equation into two words: **surrender** and **trust**.

1. The word "**surrender**" scares many people, probably because they associate it with giving up, settling, or going along with something they didn't choose. No, "surrender"

here is not equivalent to "weakness" - quite the opposite. It is about *accepting* the things we can't change and relinquishing control.

Have you had a major crush on someone yet? I'm talking *major*. If not, you will. And if so, you know what it's like to want something so badly that it hurts. Notice how it becomes toxic when you cling to something or someone this badly - often turning the other person off completely! Trying to control situations in this manner rarely works. It ends up creating needless pain and suffering. Or worse.

On the other end of the spectrum, you could try dropping your feelings altogether, telling yourself things like "It'll never happen" or "I don't care if they like me or not" (lies!). This is a form of self-denial, and it doesn't work either. By completely letting go, you deny yourself of ever having what you want. You deny yourself of the *possibilities*.

This is one scenario out of the infinite where a degree of surrender is advisable. But how do you know when to surrender or actively pursue a situation?

2. That's where **trust** comes in. Trust is the safety net that allows us to let go without fear. It's also our security that whatever is meant to be will come to us at the right time and place. And it's intrinsically tied to our beliefs, faith, and the path of least resistance...hmmm...

Again, the Universe works in mysterious ways. And by developing unwavering trust in the powers that be, you will see time and time again that, somehow, things work out for you. Even if it doesn't look that way immediately, understand that your surrender and trust have initiated the process. You have delegated your "problem" to the Universe - now allow it to work its magic (this, by the way, is where most people fail, and the real meaning of "giving up").

A simple way I'm constantly reminded of this is when driving on a crowded highway. (Maybe this isn't the optimal analogy for a teenager without a license yet, but I'm going with it anyway.) Often, I suddenly realize that my exit is approaching much quicker than I thought. Well, that's fine when the roads are clear. But it can be *highly* stressful knowing you must get over multiple lanes surrounded by bumper-to-bumper traffic going 70+ mph! Sometimes, it even looks *impossible* - a wall of cars blocking your path, a few huge trucks you can't see past, and less than a quarter mile to the exit. It's moments like these that I relinquish control: "I surrender - all is right. I trust that the Universe operates flawlessly. I am always exactly where I need to be - in the perfect place at the perfect time." And sure enough, each time, I'm amazed at how gracefully it clears or other drivers let me over. It's almost like time and space have expanded the highway for me, or the sea has parted! This might be a small example, but its meaning is potent.

Take a moment and look back at some of the scarier moments you've had and the anxieties, doubts, and fears surrounding those moments. You overcame them all, and here you are, are you not? You've undoubtedly grown from these experiences - you can probably even *laugh* at some of them now. But at the time, it felt like the end of the world. It may have seemed like things were impossible or insurmountable. In reality, your **grasp for control** created the illusion of difficulty.

Now back to something a little less intense, like that crush. Hold on loosely, but don't let go. Surrender and trust in the Universe, your higher power, or yourself. Play it cool - it's a good look! Then watch something beautiful happen: calm, peace, and (most importantly) **love** take the wheel. And love does not grasp, force, or control. It accepts, surrenders, and trusts the process. What is meant for you is already yours.

#69: DON'T BATTLE ANYTHING (THE SEESAW OF WAR)

I know this seems counterintuitive at first. It's impressed upon us to "fight for what we want," "conquer our demons," etc. But the fact is, fighting against something only creates more of it. This is one of the laws of nature and ties right into "paying attention." We constantly see people standing up for their beliefs - whether rioting and fighting the system or tackling smaller-scale disagreements. They fight passionately, and my heart truly goes out to them. The desire for *change* and *good* is typically pure, but we must realize that we can't fight fire with fire if we want to change a situation effectively. We also can't fight fire by dousing it with gasoline! You can't bring energy "A" to arena "A" and then expect the result to be "B." Stay with me - it's simpler than you think.

> *"I was once asked why I don't participate in anti-war demonstrations. I said that I will never do that, but as soon as you have a pro-peace rally, I'll be there."*
>
> — MOTHER THERESA

It's impossible to win playing by the rules of the opposition, and Mother Theresa knew this. That's an outdated way of thinking, and we must come to terms with the fact that it's *not* effective.

We have to play a different game with different rules. Energy patterns show that fighting against something we don't want is equivalent to pushing a **pendulum** back and forth. The pendulum cannot continue to swing without someone else "playing the game" - or shoving it back in the opposite direction. The pendulum *needs* someone else to play in order to exist and survive!

I came up with another analogy: a seesaw. Granted, you aren't still playing on seesaws (and if you are, that's totally cool) - but let's use Mother Theresa's war analogy since it's easy to grasp and take to the playground anyways.

So here we are with this "Seesaw of War." Now, place a kid on one side - this kid is all about arguing...violence...anger...hatred. He has claimed this seesaw. And he needs his seesaw to move because that's the only way it has any real enticement or power. So he starts running his mouth, riling up the other kids. Eventually, a brave soul emerges - we'll call him the "Defender of Peace." And this DOP decides he's had enough of the KOW (King of War? Kid of War? I don't know...it's ridiculous). He jumps on the other side of the seesaw to defend his beliefs and peace-loving classmates. And now we've got a giant spectacle - both sides going up and down, two kids yelling back and forth, others cheering it on, lots of squeaking - but no peace accomplished.

So how do we create peace if that's what we desire? How do we stop war if we can't fight it? *We play on a different seesaw.* We have to empower and embody what we **want** - and through that, what we *don't* desire fades away. We deprive the things we don't want of our energy, our power - our attention. We stop feeding it; stop watering it. And occasionally, that KOW might even realize that the "Seesaw of Peace" is the place to be and join.

This goes for **anything** we want to change - enemies, relationships, circumstances, or qualities in ourselves. You've got to adopt a mentality of supporting what you love rather than battling what you don't. Throughout your journeys from now on, do your best to remember this axiom: *"Whatever you* resist persists." I have found it to be highly accurate and helpful. I'm not saying that if you join a peace rally, it will stop the war. Global issues such as war are immense and deeply rooted in mass consciousness. But the principle remains, and it's a principle that must start on a *personal level* to have any hope of building momentum. So start by being an example in your own life, and let the ripple effect take its course. Create that **purposeful** pendulum!

"Be the change you wish to see in the world."

— MAHATMA GANDHI

****The seesaw story is another one that almost didn't make the cut. But it made me laugh, so I figured it would be well worth it if it got you to crack just a little smile.****

#70: BE A BUFFALO

I was cleaning my floor the other week, listening to a podcast, when I came across this fantastic analogy. I've known its meaning, but I'd never heard it expressed so interestingly. I realized right away that it would be perfect for - *you!*

As I understand it, there's a section of the western United States (Colorado, to be exact) where cows and buffaloes live side-by-side. And as storms typically roll in over the Rocky Mountains to the west, an interesting "phenomenon" occurs regarding the reactions and behavior of these two animals.

When the cows sense a storm approaching, they instinctually run east - *away* from the storm. And as they run away, the storm naturally follows them overhead, only maximizing their discomfort and frustration. Essentially, the cows are extending their time in the storm! They think they're running *from* it, but they're actually running **with** it.

Now, buffaloes do the exact opposite. Oddly enough, they run **into** the storm. I don't know whether this is higher wisdom or something built into their DNA. But I do know that by facing the storm head-on, they move through it quickly - effectively minimizing their discomfort and frustration.

Can you see where this is going?

We all face "storms" - they're a part of life. Storms can come in the form of arguments, breakups, illnesses, family issues, financial issues, and emotional distress, to name a few. And all too often, we react like the cows - running away from our problems and allowing them to linger overhead. We maximize our pain and drag it out, typically because, like the cows, we don't know any better.

Well, now you do.

Although we don't have control over all stormy situations, we can control *when* and *how* we respond to them - and in which direction we go. Like the buffalo, choosing to face the storm *directly* minimizes our time spent in distress and demonstrates and strengthens two outstanding qualities: **resilience** and **leadership**. Remember: *storms move too*. What if you practiced moving into and *through* your next "storm"? Try it on something small, and you'll start to understand. Next time you have awkward tension with a friend or family member, be bold and take quick action. Step out of your comfort zone and face it head-on. That little bit of initiative will take you farther than you can imagine. You'll never be a cow again.

It reminds me of eating the frog - you know, tackling the day's most challenging task first? It's the same concept: bold action in the face of uncomfortable situations. Optimizing that which you have control of. I guess when it comes down to it, I'm suggesting you become a frog-eating buffalo.

#71: SLEEP ON IT (PART 2)

We discussed problem-solving while sleeping in hack #13, but I'd like to expand on it. You can use the power of the subconscious to do virtually *anything* while you sleep. I've built this little "trick" into my daily routine, and it's changed my life. It never even used to cross my mind that the state I fell asleep in could affect…well, anything!

To recap: You are asleep roughly one-third of your life, but your subconscious **never** sleeps. It keeps you breathing, pumps blood, digests food, and controls body temperature. Likewise, it continues to work out problems, find solutions, and run whatever "program" you feed it.

What is it you truly want? Is there a burning question you'd like answered, an outcome you'd love to create, or a situation you'd like to shift? You can sleep on ANY problem, question, or desire. At the very least, you can project the overall energy for the next day. Don't just use this technique to solve problems – make it a ritual. Build it into your life. Use it to *carve out your visions*.

Take advantage of this opportunity! As you quiet down every night, right before falling asleep, go into an intense focus on the subject at hand. **Set your intention.** This is a form of meditation. Keep your body as still as possible and your eyes closed. When you redirect the energy of the five senses, ALL of that energy goes to the mind (very cool)! The key is to *fall asleep while in the desired state.*

There is one thing you should always avoid: falling asleep in a mental state that *doesn't* serve you. Have you heard the phrase "Never go to bed angry"? This is valid because anger and frustration will continue to play through your mind while you sleep, keeping the cycle going till you wake. The same is true for stress, anxiety, and other negative states. Therefore, always be aware of your thoughts and overall emotional condition before passing out.

If there are some nights you have trouble with this, or you find the delta brain waves creeping in too quickly (i.e., you're falling asleep too fast), **gratitude** is a super effective and easy tool to use. Gratitude will immediately shift your state of being and program the subconscious to reflect that while you sleep. It looks something like this:

"Thank you for my health and the health of my loved ones...thank you for a home and a bed to sleep in...thanks for a great day and for all of my friends...thanks for Derek T Freeman and his awesome books...thank you for finally getting that "Let Me Sleep on It" song by Meatloaf out of my head...thank you for clean water, air, and working appliances...thank you for...for... zzz zzz zzz..."

#72: KNOW THAT YOU KNOW NOTHING

"A fool thinks himself to be wise, but a wise man knows himself to be a fool."

— WILLIAM SHAKESPEARE

Do you know: There are things we *know* we don't know, but also things we *don't* know we don't know? Of course, you don't know - because you don't even *know* you don't know!

Admitting and accepting our "ignorance" is one of the most powerful things we can do; best to understand this now!

Come to terms with the fact that there is *so* much to learn and understand that it's beyond comprehension. Realizing our own lack of knowledge motivates us to continue learning, exploring, and growing. The people primed for growth, expansion, and high wisdom are those who understand that they will always be learning yet **never** know it all.

"Everything we hear is an opinion, not a fact. Everything we see is a perspective, not the truth."

— MARCUS AURELIUS

Never be satisfied with what you know, or *think* you know - because even the things you feel 100% confident about are likely an **illusion**. Let's look at a few examples:

1)" The earth is flat." This might sound ridiculous now (well, for most people), but for centuries it was widely accepted and believed as *fact* (Blakemore 2017).

2)" The sun revolves around the earth." Another "fact" - oh, until the 1500s when it was proven to be the opposite (Riebeek 2009).

3) Try this one on for size: Quantum physics proved "nonlocality" in 2022 (Garisto, D 2022). That means things that appear solid to us don't have a "fixed" position in time and space. They may only exist in "information" - appearing once

we become aware of them through our very limited five senses (Urdaneta 2022).

That's right, even EINSTEIN WAS WRONG - and there are TONS of these examples. Take the most elementary things you are **sure** to be "real": I promise they are not what they seem. You might think you know exactly what a tree is, a table, a bird, or a car. But these things are not solid at all. YOU are not solid at all. Broken down to the core of an atom, over 99% of *everything* is made up of space (English 2020). Our senses merely turn things into understandable "symbols" so that our brains can process and compartmentalize the data (like a zip file). In other words, what we think we see is not even *close* to reality. Physicists will never lose their jobs because theories will endlessly evolve - forever dancing around but never actually touching the **truth**. What else do we assume is a fact that, in reality, is simply the *smoke and mirrors* of the Universe?

"A mind is like a parachute. It doesn't work if it is not open."

— FRANK ZAPPA

Life is a phenomenon much bigger than you and I. The cosmos were here long before us and will remain long after us - and they will do just fine. There is clearly an intelligence far beyond anything we can ever grasp in our physical bodies. By accepting this - taking in ALL sides, ALL perspectives, ALL ideas, as simply *parts of the whole* - our intelligence will become **super-alert**. Ironically, we will gain more wisdom than ever before.

After reading this, doesn't your tiny little world and all the things you're "sure of" seem, maybe, a bit silly? At some point, you will have to accept the fact that life is one giant **paradox**. It's wild that every single one of us is absolutely nothing yet infinitely everything at the same time. You don't have to try and wrap your head around that. All you need to do is keep an open mind. Stay humble. Maintain the curiosity of a child! Know that you know nothing.

#73: THE PRESENT (READ WHEN READY!)

And now we come to the end of this little "journey," full circle, to find ourselves in the same place we started: the all-encompassing, inescapable present moment. You thought we just went down the rabbit hole, right? *Wrong.* **This** is the rabbit hole - the "red pill." Once it's seen, it can't be unseen! In other words, there's no turning back. I may be making a leap in saying this, but I don't think teenagers are given enough credit. I believe some, if not all, crave something a bit deeper than adults typically acknowledge. And I promise there will be an application for all of this. But fair warning: it gets a little dense. So buckle up!

> "Nothing has happened in the past; it happened in the Now. Nothing will ever happen in the future; it will happen in the Now."
>
> — ECKHART TOLLE

I don't expect you to actualize this notion yet fully. But I do think, at some point, you should read Eckhart's book "The Power of Now." Everyone should. I read it at 29, and I can say that it changed my life in profound ways. I am surely not yet at his level when it comes to writing, but I'm going to do my best - Derek T Freeman style.

I want you to slow down and notice something within. Notice that no matter where your thoughts go, you will always, without fail, still be in the present moment. And this is the inherent gift that's always right under our noses. In many ways, this is life's hidden truth - the goldmine.

It's so simple that it's easy to miss: **all you are is now**. You will never be any more, and you will never be any less. Every moment you've ever experienced, and *will* ever experience, will be in the present. And life is just a string of moments. To take it further, "you" are not even a noun - you're a *verb*. When you break yourself down to the truest form - your most authentic nature - you become something so effortless: the **act** of consciousness. You become the *awareness-ing*.

The inherent problem of humanity is that we live in, and identify with, our thoughts. The mind creates a "self" that we assert, defend, and protect - a cycle of recurring emotions, behaviors, and beliefs called the "ego." Now don't get me wrong, the ego plays its part - it would be almost impossible to function on planet Earth without it! But there is a point here that I would like to get across because **I don't believe it's adequately conveyed to young adults - yet I certainly think you are smart enough for it:**

The ego is valuable, yes. But it's a piece of the puzzle, not the *whole* puzzle. It's a "broken off" sense of self. The danger arises when the puzzle piece is unaware of the big picture and operates *as* the whole. In other words, when we live entirely from our thoughts (or ego) - *when we mistake the part for the whole* - we become separated from what we **really** are. So, what is this "whole," then? It's the driving, universal force of **everything**. The Source. The "field" of consciousness. Some call it God - the Divine. The words don't matter. What matters is that you are a **unique feature** of this whole.

(I'll interject here that this is what I, and many before me, have come to know. Highly religious people might call it heresy, and hardcore scientists might scoff at it. I would say this concept of "one-ness" is a beautiful marriage of science and religion - it doesn't reject either. But I'm not here to say "I'm right" - I'm here to encourage an open mind. I want YOU to have more perspective to decide for yourself what makes sense.)

You can play with this idea in different ways to better grasp it. I like to think about balloon animals. Let's say I was twisted up as a dog (I can't be *all* about cats). In the mirror, I would look like a dog. I would start acting like a dog, playing the part of what I assumed to be. Others would also see me as a dog and probably think I was cute and play with me. But a higher level of understanding would eventually tell me that I am not a dog at all - I'm a *piece of rubber filled with air.* Now imagine if you were a giant knot in a rope. From the smaller perspective, you **are** the knot. From a higher perspective, though, you can see the truth: you are the **whole rope**. The knot was just a temporary disguise - an illusion.

We now know that our TRUE selves don't exist in the past, future, or ego. Therefore, the only way to access the truth, the whole, the big picture - is through the **present**.

"If you are depressed you are living in the past. If you are anxious you are living in the future. If you are at peace you are living in the present."

— LAO TZU

Let's try a little experiment. Think about a time in your recent past that you remember as "magical" or "perfect." A time that was so full of fun, freedom, and newness. Maybe your last vacation or a trip with some friends. Think about how badly you wish you could do it again - wish you could BE there again. Think about all the good food you ate, games you played, great people you got to be around, or sites you saw. Got it? Take a minute and sit with those feelings.

Now, I want you to STOP thinking from the present - and think about how you felt **during** that time. Was it as amazing as the memory is? Be real. Maybe you were full and lethargic some of the time because you overate? Did you feel *bored* some of the time - did your thoughts wander? Perhaps you were anticipating the next vacation day or driving around and not doing anything spectacular. If you're being honest with yourself, did it feel as magical at the moment as the memory feels now? Or was it just *normal* - spurts of good feelings amidst other everyday concerns?

If you were **fully** present throughout that time, then perhaps the answer is "YES - it was pure magic!" But most of the time, for most of us, our minds tend to glorify the past and future - to pull out and condense the best or worst moments or expectations and use them in comparison to the present. All the while, we're missing out on - you guessed it, the NOW. We constantly trade the *present* for the *mind*, the **truth** for the **lie**.

So how does this *actually impact you*? Although it may not feel like it, I'm not just trying to mess with your head and tangle up your brain. This wisdom affects you in ways you can't even fathom yet - and that's why I think it should be introduced at an earlier age. Allow me to explain how living in the moment - how *identifying as* the moment - can enhance your existence in far-reaching ways:

1) What's another word for "present"? *Gift.* To deny the present is to miss out on life's greatest **gift**. When you start living less and less in the past or a projected future, synchronicities, serendipities, and other blessings become regular occurrences. When you align yourself with the Now, everything starts falling into place.

2) As you stop living solely from the mind, you realize it's all just been patterning and programming - not the **real** you. You begin to dissolve that low level of being. You expand your consciousness and awareness of who you are. You grow. This opens doors to the places *"you don't even know you don't know about."* Putting the mind in its proper place will also improve every relationship in your life.

3) What's another way to say the plural of "present"? *Presence.* The power of the **Now** places you directly into Source - or, Divine Presence. Although this Presence is always there, we "pinch it out" by living in our heads, making it much harder to access. Access to this higher power brings sharper intuition, guidance, clarity, contentment, peace, and a higher life experience on every level.

"Mindfulness" is a buzzy term these days, but it's the same thing as being **fully present**. That, to me, is true spirituality - true higher power. And it might seem like I've been trash-talking the past and the future, but let me assure you of something: they have gifts for us, too! **The past *teaches* us**. If we let it, it can even become our *greatest* teacher. It's only through the compass of the past that we can direct our way forward. And **the future shows us that we don't have control** - therefore, it teaches us surrender, faith, and trust (revisit #67 & 68 for a reminder of how powerful these are). The future is also full of **wonder** - it allows us to aspire and set meaningful goals.

Finally, by encouraging you to be present, I'm not suggesting you don't work towards anything. We all inherently want and *need* to imagine, create, and grow! But we want to do it grounded in the present, knowing this is our place of power - our truth. I believe that, as humans, life should be a graceful tightrope walk between "being" and "becoming."

You may not be able to wrap your head around this yet. You may not even be interested in it. It certainly takes a level of maturity to contemplate these concepts. But guess what? *This is part of adulting!* Digging deeper, expanding further, and ascending higher - **evolving**. Despite what some other books may tell you, it's not *all* about working, cooking, and cleaning - sorry. But don't feel that you have to force it. Don't rush it, either. Explore to find your truth. You will come to it, or it will come to you - at the perfect time. Your only job is to stay open and receptive to it.

To conclude, the paradox of presence is that it's infinitely complicated and dumbfoundingly simple at the same time. But hey, don't forget: life *is* one giant paradox. Could it be that our ability to hold para*dox* equals our ability to hold para...*dise*?

With that, I'll leave you one final quote to wrap up this section:

"The more wisdom you attain and the more conscious you become, the crazier you will appear to others."

— UNKNOWN

7

JOB & CAREER

"It takes courage to grow up and become who you really are."

— E.E CUMMINGS

The good news: now that we've gone super deep into the rabbit hole, "Job and Career" will seem like a piece of cake! Well, maybe in reading. I assure you, everything from here on out is *not* a piece of cake. Regardless, **independence** is what the teen years have been leading up to. The bird must fly the coup. Although your mom says you should live with her forever, trust me - even *she* wants you to get a job and move out (at some point).

Your journey is just beginning - it's time to start thinking about what you want to do with the rest of your time on this planet! Your career will shape your life for many years, so it should undoubtedly lay the groundwork for success. But it's a balancing act. Yes, you'll need to make sure you have a job that pays the bills - but you'll also want one that is fulfilling and allows you to grow purposefully. We all deserve to **love** our lives; otherwise, what's the point (hence "Sur-Thrival Guide")?

I'll be completely transparent with you: It's April 2023, and things are a little...crazy. AI is set to take off, job descriptions are uniquely changing, and technology is rapidly advancing, amongst other social and political disruptions. I assume things in the next few years will transform before our eyes. With that in mind, I would much rather impart **timeless** wisdom than advice that eventually becomes dated. So, like with the rest of this book, I'll be very intentional about bringing you the best of both worlds in this chapter: the essential "big picture" insight and the real, tangible techniques that work NOW.

HACK #74: GO YOUR OWN WAY

"We must let go of the life we have planned, so as to accept the one that is waiting for us."

— JOSEPH CAMPBELL

I love this quote because it reminds me of how curious, spontaneous, and exciting life is. But for this particular hack's sake, let's slightly alter it: "We must let go of the life **they** have planned, so as to accept the one that is waiting for us."

You're going to reach a point when, inevitably, everyone will gladly interject their opinion on your future: what schools to apply to, what jobs to get, where to live, etc. You'll hear all about what you "should" do, what "they would do," or what they *did* that worked for *them*. You'll receive TONS of advice - and though it will come from a good place, it may not all be right for **you**. Others mean well, but they aren't living your life - you are. On top of that, many of these people (aside from immediate family) won't even be around to see you live that life - and that's ok! Some people are only meant to be in your life for so long. Think about what it takes for a rocket ship to reach its destination: once it hits a certain altitude, it must detach from the boosters that got it there. That same metaphor applies to the suggestions surrounding you and the "detaching" of what might hinder you from reaching your unique destination.

"Always be a first-rate version of yourself, instead of a second-rate version of someone else."

— JUDY GARLAND

Story time. It was my senior year of high school, and I was about three years into starting my band (aka practicing every night in our parents' basement with only a few live shows under our belt). I wasn't internally ready to pursue college at this point - I needed to see where the creative path could lead. Also, I had *no clue* what else to do - nothing besides music even appealed to me! This was a confusing time because I knew I needed to start thinking about a "stable" career in case things didn't work out as I envisioned. You could say I had one foot in the "real world" and one foot in my "dream world."

One of the technical classes I took during this time was called CADD (Computer-Aided Design and Drafting). Although it didn't overly thrill me, I was good at it. All my school counselors and relatives pushed me to pursue it - rightfully so and with good intentions. It seemed *safe* - I had everyone's approval and could see myself juggling that and the band. I even had a job secured for me after high school ended!

So right after I graduated, I started my new job. It was a standard 40-hour work week - Monday through Friday, 9 am to 5 pm, with a perfectly scheduled half-hour lunch in the middle of each day. It looked promising initially: I sat down and did my work for eight hours, and no one bothered me. I would go home, have band practice, eat dinner, sleep, and do it all again. Wash, rinse, repeat.

But after a few months of this routine, it started to wear on me. My back hurt from sitting all day. I noticed I was running through the motions of the job but thinking about songs and lyrics the whole time. Time went by slower...and slower. Glancing at the clock became torturous. As the weeks passed, it only continued to drain me - physically, mentally, and creatively. *It drained my soul.* I began to experience what can only be described as a "holding pattern," in which I didn't feel like I was going anywhere. My whole life felt like it was on hold, and that's because it was. I was working hard, but nothing felt tangible or meaningful to me. I rarely use the "H" word, but: I HATED IT.

You get the point. But to sum up the end of the story: I quit my job, toured for many years with the band, played in front of hundreds of thousands of people, put out over six albums, and still make music today. Most notably, I don't regret *going my own way.*

> *"Everyone you meet always asks if you have a career, are married, or own a house as if life was some kind of grocery list. But no one asks if you are happy."*
>
> — HEATH LEDGER

I feel like I have to say this: I'm not encouraging you to quit a job or take a chance on something risky just to do it. I'm encouraging you to follow your heart. Some people crave stability and routine. Some do very well with a desk job. College might not have been for me then, but it may be **just** what you need. Also, not everyone is built for the uncertainties of entrepreneurship. Regardless of what you choose, let the choice be yours - not someone else's. And then be ready to go all in.

In a nutshell: whatever you do, stay true to **you**. Listen to all of the advice, but learn the art of extracting only what truly resonates. This is another major part of adulting: **making your own decisions.** But that also doesn't mean you have to be alone in this.

(To be continued in #78...)

#75: DIVERSIFY NOW, STREAMLINE LATER

Now that we've established this chapter's "ethos," let's assume you haven't graduated high school yet. Believe it or not, the reality is that you don't have to know your exact career path right now. Remember that buffet, the one with the asparagus you didn't like? Well, it's time to partake in it.

And by "buffet," I mean the wide variety of jobs, experiences, and opportunities out there. This is truly the time to dabble in as much as possible! Take some interesting classes, volunteer at a local charity, join a club or sports team, or develop your entrepreneurial skills. Push yourself to try something completely different, even if it's just an experiment - you never know what might spark your curiosity.

Summer jobs are an excellent way to develop social skills, confidence, and connections (let alone make money). I've often heard it recommended that everyone have at *least* one customer service job at some point in their life, and I couldn't agree more. Often, these life lessons are more valuable than the traditional classroom experience.

By diversifying your experiences, you can narrow down what truly lights you up. For instance, you might discover through volunteer work that you enjoy being in charge, getting creative with advertising, and interacting with various people. In this case, a career in **marketing** may be for you. On the other hand, you might work a desk job for a while and be led to realize that you crave something much more **active**. Sometimes *contrast* can be the BEST teacher when it comes to discovering yourself. And nothing is permanent right now, making the timing even better. Again - you want to think of each venture as an experiment.

The icing on the cake? The more diverse your resume is, the better you'll come across when applying for bigger jobs!

So maybe you should *try* the asparagus. Grab a little chicken...a few bites of potato salad. I hear the shrimp is on point today. Fill that plate up! When you reach the end, you'll better understand your true passions and how they can be streamlined into your career success.

#76: RESPOND TO AI WITH HI (NOT WHAT YOU THINK!)

As I mentioned earlier, AI-based technology is profoundly changing the face of the workplace. And as with any rapidly advancing technology, some skeptics will worry about its implications for the labor market. The truth is that AI will only continue to change the way we work, and it's not going anywhere. So, what does this mean for you as a job-seeker? How will you respond to this challenge?

You may think the obvious response to "artificial intelligence" would be upgraded "human intelligence" - that you'll stand out from the competition by learning, memorizing, and studying hard. But guess what? You can't beat AI at its own game. We've got to come to terms with the fact that we cannot compete with its calculation speed and that there are going to be jobs that AI will inevitably dominate.

Instead, we must ask: "What is the one thing AI *can't* do?" And that is: **be human**. That's right - the way to stay ahead of AI is to be *more* human. Specifically, we need to improve our **Human Interaction**.

Instead of focusing only on the technical knowledge and know-how that robots might be able to do better, you would be wise to develop *real* interpersonal skills and your unique abilities. It is suggested that concentrating on the following skills early on will help you get ahead of your competitors and succeed in a workplace that is constantly changing:

- public speaking
- influencing
- marketing
- sales
- customer service
- project management
- delegating
- networking
- problem-solving

(Murphy, P. 2021)

Perfect your people skills! I predict the "human experience" will become more valuable to employers, employees, customers, and businesses in the coming years. The more AI does for us, the more our inherent skills will be in demand. So don't fear AI - do what it can't. You can even use it to your advantage in the process. Like any powerful tool, it can be used for good or evil - just like a kitchen knife can be used to prepare a tasty dish or to harm someone. It all depends on the user. How can AI work *for* you?

#77: NAIL ANY INTERVIEW

The interview process is almost inevitable. But did you know there are ways to vastly improve your chances of getting *any* job that may be right for you? I'll assume you can figure out the basics for yourself (dressing appropriately, being punctual, etc.). What I'm going to teach you is more in-depth. Follow these steps to secure a position that benefits you AND your potential employer:

1) Do Your Homework. The homework never ends, does it? This is *very* important, though - that's why it's number one. Ensure you thoroughly research any organization or company you plan to interview with. There are many resources online that can help with this. Some research basics include reading up-to-date news articles about the business, familiarizing yourself with its "mission" and values, and getting in touch with current or former employees (alumni groups or networking organizations can provide great connections). Being well-versed and knowledgeable about the company will earn you major points.

2) Follow the Statistics. Specific times are more favorable for you to schedule an interview if you have the option. For instance, you ideally want to avoid being interviewed first, last, *or* in the middle of the day. Shoot for the slot right before noon time - late morning, roughly 10 am to 11:30 am. The weekly timing reflects that, too: aim for the spot right before the midpoint (Tuesday, in a perfect world). This is just my cheat sheet for you - if you'd like the psychology behind it, feel free to research the references (Zhang 2020).

3) Know Thyself. Any interviewer will ask you about yourself, and often they will lead with that. It's best to prepare a few short speaking points so you're ready when the time comes. Brainstorm the following questions to develop an impressive "summary" of yourself: What are your strengths and weaknesses? What do you value in yourself and others? What sort of things have you accomplished in school or a previous job? What interests or hobbies do you have? What experiences have shaped you? (Bonus points for a quick story about overcoming a challenge or learning from a mistake.)

4) The Reverse Interview. Instead of going into the interview thinking of yourself as the one being interviewed, think of it as an opportunity to interview *them*. Nurture the mindset that **you are valuable**: Does the company fit with your values and beliefs? Does it provide you with the potential to develop and grow? Would you be proud to tell your family and friends you work here? Is this something you could see yourself doing for the foreseeable future? Establish some questions ahead of time that YOU have for THEM. Within a few minutes of the interview, you can feel whether or not it "vibes" with you. Keep your standards high - you have permission to be picky.

5) Leave a Lasting Impression. Finish the process as gracefully and professionally as you began it. Give a firm handshake (people remember that!), express genuine enthusiasm for the opportunity, and thank the interviewer(s). Take it further by sending a "thank you" note, email, or phone call (whichever is more appropriate) within 24 hours of the interview. That extra effort will keep you at the top of the list when hiring decisions are made.

#78: THE ART OF LETTING PEOPLE IN

I generally emphasize "trusting yourself" and "going your own way." Understand that this is because, in my observation, the scales tend to tip the other way early on in life. When you're in high school, things can be so overwhelming that the "security" of following the crowd often feels irresistible.

But here's the thing: You can't go through life alone, and there's a balance there that I'd like to help you achieve. We need other people for many reasons, and learning from their experiences of transitioning into the "real world" is a huge part of that. No, other people don't have to be the ones who tell you what's right and wrong - but they *can* provide helpful advice and offer reference points from which you can make your own decisions.

Like diversifying early on with job experience, now is the time to learn from as many seasoned adults as possible. Here are some ways you can collect the data to make intelligent, informed choices when it comes to college or career:

- "Interview" family, extended family, and trusted neighbors for their advice and potential shortcuts. Teachers can also play a big part if you've developed that relationship with them.
- Read as many books and articles as you can about role models you admire. Follow their socials and learn from their tips.
- Consider talking to a career specialist. This can be done in person or online, and chances are your parents would be happy to pay for a session.
- Set up a profile on LinkedIn to ask for advice in your field of interest. There are thousands upon thousands of successful people on there.
- This can be a bit humbling, but if you don't get a job you applied for, ask for some constructive criticism on *why* they didn't hire you. That right there is a shortcut and a half!

There's an ocean of knowledge around you - it would be foolish not to take advantage of it. Who else can you learn from? What other resources are at your disposal that can help propel you to success while saving you tons of time and frustration?

#79: DON'T BE BEST, BE UNRIVALED

"Do not go where the path may lead; go instead where there is no path and leave a trail."

— RALPH WALDO EMERSON

Fighting your way to the top - what a rat race. That concept never excited me. There's always going to be someone better than you, period. More than that, once you reach the "top," everyone else is constantly gunning for your position. Where's the security in that?

No matter how good you are, to be the "best" means you will always be competing. Alternately, the more unique or innovative you are, the more valuable you will be - and the more job security you will have.

It might be wise to aim for being a big fish in a little pond rather than a big fish in a *big* pond. Yes, you still want to be "big" - if "big" means good at what you do - but your surroundings can make all the difference regarding your preservation.

Let me give a couple of examples. Imagine you were in college when virtual reality gaming was coming out. And say, at the time, you were pursuing a *general* gaming career. If you instead were to focus on becoming one of the few experts in VR - a very specified niche of gaming - people would be banging down your door once it hit the mainstream. You would already have been established, far ahead of the curve and any competition.

Think about podcasting. It's huge now but was virtually unheard of in the early 2000s. What if you were an entrepreneur with the foresight to jump on board early, becoming a well-established podcaster before it blew up? You could have set yourself up for way more success than if you had waited till everyone else hopped on the bandwagon.

This doesn't just apply to leading in new technology - it's a way of thinking. You don't need to reinvent the wheel (or invent *anything*) if you don't have the mind for it. But it would help if you started to think outside the box. If you are interested in a specific field, how can you effectively "niche down"? You could specialize in vegan cooking instead of just being a chef. Or you could focus on quantum computing instead of just being a programmer. How might it benefit you to become proficient in a **specific** field that is way less saturated?

Seek out and pay attention to opportunities "off the beaten path." If you were to give your job description to family or friends, would they instantly know what it was, or would they be scratching their heads? Shoot for the latter! That is the power of being unrivaled: because you are not competing with the masses, you become an **asset** to those who need your skills. In some cases, you can become the *only* asset - which is true personal power.

#80: SEEK DELAYED GRATIFICATION (PART 2)

We discussed the essence of delayed gratification and how it applies to money appreciation and growing it long-term. Now, let's bring the concept of delayed gratification into your job, career, and even broader contexts.

The idea of delayed gratification goes beyond finances and applies to *anything* that you truly desire. As human beings, we tend to want immediate results - but this can be a trap. Start thinking of gratification in a new light. Nothing extraordinary, deep, meaningful, or truly fulfilling is ever created instantly - think about that! A good everyday example of this is a house plant. When you first buy it, the pot might be full of soil and nothing else - no color, texture, or apparent beauty. But you nurture it. You feed it. You know what it could become. And soon, you find that same pot can sprout something magnificent with the right amount of water, sunlight, care, and time. Your nourishing it will *significantly* enhance the outcome when it blooms and comes to life. Sure, you could buy a fake plant (instant gratification) - it might even last forever! But guess what? It's plastic.

Lifeless. Unfulfilling. And it will more or less lose its appeal in a few days, gather dust, and fade into its surroundings.

In certain aspects of life, instant gratification can be a good thing. Music, movies, and food are some sources of pleasure that can provide an immediate "lift" and a sense of joy. Dancing, sports, meditation, and other arts can be forms of instant gratification while also nurturing the spirit. But when you start relying on the quick-fix mentality for everything - or use it strictly to avoid pain - it can lead to a shallow, unsatisfying life.

Your career is like that plant, and you'll want to view it with the long-term in mind. If you end up an entrepreneur - or working for yourself in *any* capacity - delayed gratification will be a **requirement**. You must be willing to weather the stormy seas, stay the course, and trust that it will yield its benefits in due time. This path is only meant for some, as it rarely provides immediate security and often involves many risks. And if you choose to work for someone else, delayed gratification still applies. You'll want to focus on developing skills and bettering yourself, creating a work-life balance you're happy with, building relationships, and advancing your career. This takes time, energy, and effort - but the compensation can be massive if done correctly.

So, once you've diversified your job experiences, realized what you *don't* want, and honed in on what you're meant for - water it. Nurture it. Give it time. Know that the degree to which it will pay off is unparalleled and that you will be rewarded for your dedication.

#81: THE ULTIMATE SUCCESS SECRET

We've scratched this surface in the "Money" section. No matter what career you choose, what form money takes, or what time period it may be, success will ALWAYS depend on just one thing: that you **provide value to others**.

Too simple? Well, the truth always *is* simple! But that doesn't mean most people recognize and abide by it.

The axiom "What you put into life is what you get out of it" doesn't get ANY simpler. But how many people do you see utilizing this in all their relationships, responsibilities, and endeavors?

If we all followed the mind-numbingly elementary Golden Rule and treated "others as we want to be treated," the world would be *unrecognizably* better. Yet, we don't all do this, do we?

Just because something sounds basic or cliche doesn't mean it isn't vastly powerful. And "Providing value to others" is a perfect example of **simple power**.

So many people gauge "success" by the amount of money in their bank account. And although that might be part of it, it's putting the cart before the horse. When pursuing money becomes your chief aim, you become unstable and dependent on it. You live and die by the trends of the marketplace. You lose all *real* security. (Not to mention, life becomes completely hollow.)

Remember how "money is energy"? Well, "serving others" would be the action verb of that statement. When your focus is on providing value, filling a void, or improving someone's life in some way, money *has* to follow. It's as simple as directing your intention and as sure as the sun's rising. You'll *always* be wealthy. And you'll *always* be fulfilled.

The best part about this success secret is that it can be applied to every field, job, and stage in life. With so many people fixated on "acquiring," dare to be focused on "becoming." I promise you that all the material possessions in the world amount to nothing. What matters is how you affect others. You are a *verb*, remember? So set your sights on *becoming* valuable to others, and inject that mentality into your profession. Serve others, and you will be served. Easy, right?

Some of these "hacks" are just **truths** that many young people overlook - but they're hidden in plain sight! Be more brilliant and *pay attention* - it's simpler than you think.

8

BONUS - CARS!

"Have you ever noticed that anybody driving slower than you is an idiot, and anyone going faster than you is a maniac?"

— GEORGE CARLIN

I can still see my first car now - a silver 1986 Toyota Corolla Hatchback. Standard transmission. It's actually a lie to call it silver because it was more the color of **rust**. It was basically *made* of rust.

I drove that car to and from school - that's it. Making it home and up my parents' country roads *required* me always to have the pedal to the floor. Three different air fresheners dazzled the rearview mirror. And a leopard throw blanket that **never** left the vehicle decorated the back seat. You read that right.

This car probably looked (and sounded) like a nightmare to everyone else. But to me, it was pure perfection. It was a symbol of my **independence**. And I wouldn't have traded that for the world (well, maybe for a better car).

In high school, I knew nothing about cars except how to drive them. And although I still don't know much more, I *do* love them and have some powerful advice up my sleeve! But why is this section a "bonus," you might ask?

I don't know how much longer conventional gas vehicles will be around. They'll be replaced with electric, self-driving, and flying cars sooner or later. And as I touched upon in the last chapter, I'd rather not give dated information. You can learn how to change your oil or a flat tire in virtually any "life skills" book - or with a simple search online. But I know one thing that **won't** change: cars come with new levels of freedom. And with that freedom comes new levels of responsibility. And with that new responsibility, you deserve some fresh new hacks.

So no, I won't teach you how to jump-start a dead battery or fill up your windshield wiper fluid. Because these are **bonus** hacks, baby - bold, quick, sleek, and efficient. Just like your first car, no doubt.

HACK #82: HUMILITY FIRST

I know - you want a sports car or at least a *somewhat* impressive vehicle. But we can't all be blessed with that '86 Corolla right off the bat, can we? All joking aside, wanting a car that turns heads is entirely natural. Unfortunately, that's not usually a bright (or even realistic) idea the first time around. Here's what you should be looking for:

1) Affordability. You have your whole life to build up to the car of your dreams, but for now, you should focus on something within your budget. Even if you can afford it, it's not worth going into debt for a car as a teenager. And remember that a bigger engine also means more at the gas pump and higher insurance rates. Believe it or not, the "new car feeling" eventually wears off - but guess what doesn't? *The bills!*

2) Practicality. You'll be learning from many mistakes on this one - better to do that in something...humble. View this as your practice car as far as care and maintenance go. Consider a used car - this will teach you about buying and reselling on a manageable level. Also, flashy cars are more susceptible to break-ins, vandalism, and theft.

3) Safety. As a first-time driver, this is the lowest level of experience you will ever have. A safe car is paramount to anything else; you'll want something reliable. I think this whole tip goes without saying, but I wanted to be...safe.

#83: MASTER BASIC MAINTENANCE

You are correct; I did say I wouldn't teach basic maintenance. What I *will* do, however, is give you a cheat sheet of basics that you *should* learn. Come to think of it, this can be a good bonding experience with Mom or Dad (hinting at my kids if they ever read my books).

1) Check the oil level. Oil is the lifeblood of your car. Although it's typically changed every six months or so by a professional, you should still learn to check it regularly. You just look at the dipstick, right? I'm still learning this one.

2) Wipers and fluid. Your windshield wipers are vital as they're responsible for your visibility. Get in the habit of regularly inspecting the blades and monitoring the washer fluid level.

3) Tire pressure and tread. You'll want to keep your tire pressure at the correct level, as it affects fuel economy and handling. Look for potential wear or cracks on your tires regularly, and keep an eye on the tread depth (search "The Penny Test").

4) Front and rear lights. For safety reasons and to avoid getting pulled over, check your headlights, front and rear signals, brake and reverse lights, and high beams weekly to ensure they're in working order.

5) Brakes. A pro usually checks your brakes along with the oil change. Regardless, keep tabs on them by listening and feeling for any oddities in their performance.

6) Learn your warning lights. The descriptions are all in your manual! Best to learn these safely in the driveway or garage before being forced to figure it out on the road.

7) Consider an emergency service. It's hard to go wrong with a company like AAA that can offer roadside assistance whenever needed. Your parents will probably agree.

#84: PAY (WITH) ATTENTION (PART 2)

Before you get into the driver's seat of a potentially deadly weapon (aka car), you must deeply understand this: driving deserves - no, **demands** - your full attention. Unlike everyday life, where things you pay attention to materialize over time, driving's cause-and-effect is immediate - and the results can be disastrous.

Trust me - all it takes is one good scare, one split-second slam on the brakes, to straighten you out REAL quick. And that's the *good* outcome. I hope you never, **ever** have to experience the flip side of that coin. This isn't meant to scare you, but...well, yeah...I guess it is meant to scare you.

So that I'm being absolutely clear: pay attention ONLY TO DRIVING when driving. And in case that's not clear enough, here's a list of distracting things ***not*** to do while driving:

- cram five friends into your backseat
- blare music that drowns out other car horns
- mess with the radio or any screen settings
- put someone out the sunroof
- TEXT
- rev the engine at a red light
- rev the engine ever
- race
- show off in ANY way
- distract other drivers
- eat
- check yourself out in the rearview
- take selfies
- drink alcohol (do I need to say that?)

Disclaimer: It *is* possible to graduate to "eating while driving" (I have achieved this level). Maybe you'll get there one day. For now, don't risk any distractions. You'll preserve your car, license, freedom, life, and the lives of others. You'll also become more **valuable** to others the more mature, reliable, and dependable you are. Just remember this when on the road: attentive *always* trumps impressive.

#85: ¼ IS THE NEW "E"

A simple hack that has saved me from many a hardship in my teen years.

One thing you can happily go through life without *ever* having experienced is **running out of gas**. Therefore, mentally assume that "E," or "Empty," doesn't even exist - and that the 1/4 mark means you're officially out of gas.

Because you know what? That "E" is a tricky little fellow. And it will creep up on you at the **worst** of times. Don't believe me? Well, feel free to skip this hack, then. But don't come to me looking to siphon a few gallons into your gas can (if you're lucky enough to obtain one) because I'll be driving right by with my full tank and chicken sandwich.

However, if you're wise enough to incorporate this tip and *always* gas up before you hit a quarter tank, you'll permanently bypass that horrible and awkward experience.

PS - The fuller your tank is, the heavier your car is - which gains you extra traction in winter.

#86: EQUIP FOR EMERGENCIES

Having a proper emergency kit is all pros and no cons - do the work to set it up, and you won't have to think about it much until you need it. It also takes up little to no space - you can effectively hide it, so it's not an eyesore.

Granted, the need for an emergency kit was drastically higher in the days of the 1986 Corolla - modern cars are much more reliable. Also, granted, you can easily *buy* an emergency kit these days, so there isn't a need to hunt down each item and assemble it yourself (unless you'd like that). Generally, the older the vehicle, the more crucial your kit becomes. So, if you buy a used car, equipping for emergencies is a **must**.

Regardless of making or buying your kit, here are the core essentials:

- Flashlight with extra batteries
- Basic toolkit (for fixing minor issues)
- Jumper cables
- Tire repair kit (this could include a pressure gauge, sealant, jack, and even an inflator)
- Emergency flares
- Water and non-perishable snacks
- First aid kit
- Fire extinguisher
- Portable phone charger
- Blanket (the leopard throw blanket is recommended but not required)

What you put into your kit is what you'll get out of it! Remember to check specific items periodically to ensure they haven't expired. Also, your location and the season may dictate additional items such as a snow shovel, ice scraper, gloves, and sand.

PS - If you get stuck in mud or snow, you can pull your mats out of the car and wedge them under the tires to help gain traction.

#87: THE DOS AND DON'TS OF TAILGATING

Tailgating means driving too closely to another vehicle. It can be tempting to do (especially when the car in front of you is moving at a snail's pace), but it can also be hazardous. On top of that, it can place a lot of fear, stress, and anxiety on the recipient. While those things are *never* good to inflict on another, the road is arguably the **worst** place to do it.

So, the "Don'ts" of tailgating are pretty simple: don't do it! It **never** amounts to anything good. Did you know that the rear driver is usually "at fault"? That means if you're tailgating someone and THEY slam on the brakes resulting in a collision, YOU'RE generally the one that will get in trouble. Trust me when I say it's not worth playing that game! You should keep a three to four-second "gap" between yourself and other vehicles - this allows enough time to respond appropriately to most situations (in slippery conditions, you'll want to allow for more).

But what about the "Dos"? What do you do when you're the one being tailgated? Well, you follow these steps:

1) Don't panic! Staying calm will prevent road rage from escalating and allow you to diffuse the situation with a clear head. One thing I like to remind myself of when someone gets right up on my…bumper; is that *it's not personal. That their behavior has nothing to do with me.*

2) Stand your ground. Don't let the other driver push you out of your comfort zone. Maintain your speed if It's adequate and within the limit. They might ride you for a bit and even flash their high beams, but that's typically *all* they will do. In other words, they're not going to crash into you.

3) Don't brake too quickly. This is called "brake checking" and is never recommended as it can lead to accidents, serious injury, or even death. Sometimes, an accident can be considered your fault if you brake hard without a good reason. When braking, do it slowly and gradually to give the tailgater enough time to react.

4) Let them pass. When you have a safe opportunity, signal and pull over or to another lane so they can pass you. Try to put it out of your mind and let it go as quickly as possible. *They* will have to deal with the repercussions of their choices - not you.

#88: SEE AND BE SEEN

And finally, I leave you with this excellent rule of thumb to live (drive) by: *always position your car where it has the best chance of being seen.* Not only is this way of thinking great for safety and avoiding accidents, but it's more likely that cute people in other cars will ask you out at stoplights (I'm totally kidding, this NEVER happens. Or does it?).

Here's how you can practice "being seen":

- Stay out of others' blind spots
- Keep your headlights on any time it's not broad daylight
- Keep all lights in operating order
- Use low beams in foggy weather
- Avoid sketchy backroads or shortcuts if possible
- Use your signals
- Always park in well-lit areas

Likewise, visibility works both ways. Practice these habits to make sure YOU can always see what's going on around you:

- Always be aware of your blind spots (consider blind-spot mirrors)
- Keep your headlights on any time it's not broad daylight
- Keep all lights in operating order
- Use high beams when there's no oncoming traffic

- Keep the windows and windshields clean and free of debris
- Don't tint your windows too dark/illegally
- Use corrective eye-wear (glasses or contacts) if needed

PUT THAT "HIDDEN HACK" INTO ACTION!

You have a wealth of tools at your disposal now, which puts you in the perfect position to help someone else.

You can be the one who empowers others by taking 60 seconds to share your honest opinion of this book.

WANT TO HELP OTHERS?

Thank you again for your support. You have an incredible life ahead of you, just waiting to be discovered.

Scan the QR Code below to leave a review!

CONCLUSION

The idea for this project came from a desire to deliver something fresh and unique that would benefit you through every year of young adulthood. I've given you the best of my ability in every category which might be pertinent to you, and it feels complete - like my work here is done! I might even order myself a copy.

As you may have noticed, this writing isn't strictly for young people, even though much is specific to grade school. I always intend to put something more meaningful behind my messages, and if you've picked up on that, I salute you! I also believe that we can and SHOULD be teaching and learning more "evolved" things at younger ages. If that resonates with you, please tell others about this book. Help spread the message. Be part of this movement.

I want to hammer this home again: adulting shouldn't be synonymous with conforming, losing your personality, or getting too "serious." Becoming an adult should mean, very simply - *becoming responsible for yourself*. And that can be pretty exciting, deeply insightful, and infinitely empowering.

To wrap up: I want you to **sur-thrive**. I want you to apply this stuff and start being responsible for yourself as a human being. **But I want you to have fun and love it**. All the potential is already there, and the timing has never been better. I want others' jaws to drop when they see how autonomous (look it up) and supreme you are. Show everyone you know your worth, and make something incredible of your life - not just for you but for the world. We need it!

Ooh, one last thing! I almost forgot the final hack:

#89: Cover your mouth when you cough.

REFERENCES

A Few Requirements for a Strong Friendship. (2020, October 28). One Love Foundation. https://www.joinonelove.org/learn/5-requirements-for-a-strong-friendship/

Andriani, B. L. (2013). Uses for Vinegar. *Oprah.com.* https://www.oprah.com/home/uses-for-vinegar/all

Anxiety Centre. (2021, June 23). *Reading For 6 Minutes Reduces Stress By 68 Percent - AnxietyCentre.com.* AnxietyCentre.com. https://www.anxietycentre.com/research/reading-reduces-stress-by-68-percent/

Blakemore, E. (2017, October 6). *Christopher Columbus Never Set Out to Prove the Earth was Round.* History. https://www.history.com/news/christopher-columbus-never-set-out-to-prove-the-earth-was-round

Borowski, S. (2012, July 16). *Quantum mechanics and the consciousness connection.* AAAS. https://www.aaas.org/quantum-mechanics-and-consciousness-connection#:~:text=The%20%22observer%20effect%22%20states%20that,an%20interesting%20set%20of%20theories

Bruno, A. (2019, May 9). 12 Microwave Hacks That Will Change Your Cooking Game. *SELF.* https://www.self.com/story/microwave-cooking-hacks

Caporimo, A. (2021, September 20). 9 Life-Changing Cooking Hacks If You're New To The Kitchen. *Seventeen.* https://www.seventeen.com/life/food-recipes/a13968963/easy-cooking-hacks-for-new-cooks/

Cho, A. (2017, October 27). *Quantum experiment in space confirms that reality is what you make it.* Science. https://www.science.org/content/article/quantum-experiment-space-confirms-reality-what-you-make-it-0

Daugherty, L. (2023, March 22). 5 Ways Multitasking Is Bad for Your Mental Health (and 4 Things to Do Instead). *CNET.* https://www.cnet.com/health/mental/5-ways-multitasking-is-bad-for-your-mental-health-and-4-things-to-do-instead/

Dispenza, J. (2015). *You Are the Placebo: Making Your Mind Matter.* Hay House, Inc.

Dr, W. W. D. (2006). *The Power of Intention.* Hay House, Inc.

DriversEd.com. (n.d.). *A Few Basic Car Maintenance Tips for Teens*. https://driversed.com/resources/auto-central/teen-guide-to-basic-car-maintenance/

Dylan, S. (2023, January 9). These 17 High School Hacks Are SUPERPOWERS (Life Hacks for Students) » TeenWire.org. *TeenWire.org*. https://www.teenwire.org/high-school-hacks-and-life-hacks-for-students/

Elliott, C. (2023). 8 Money Tips For Teens So Your Future Self Will Thank You. *Listen Money Matters*. https://www.listenmoneymatters.com/money-tips-for-teenagers/

English, T. (2020, February 28). *Due to the Space inside Atoms, You Are Mostly Made up of Empty Space*. Interesting Engineering. https://interestingengineering.com/science/due-to-the-space-inside-atoms-you-are-mostly-made-up-of-empty-space

Evan. (2023, April 3). *65 Reward Ideas for Kids (And brain-science explained) - Dad Fixes Everything*. Dad Fixes Everything. https://dadfixeseverything.com/reward-ideas/

Fraser-Thill, R. (2022). When Is the Appropriate Age to Start Dating? *Verywell Family*. https://www.verywellfamily.com/is-it-normal-to-see-children-dating-3287991

Garisto, D. (2022, October 6). *The Universe Is Not Locally Real, and the Physics Nobel Prize Winners Proved It*. Scientific American. https://www.scientificamerican.com/article/the-universe-is-not-locally-real-and-the-physics-nobel-prize-winners-proved-it/#

Jazmin Tolliver, L., BA. (2021, November 23). *Health Debunked: Are Microwaves Bad for Your Health?* GoodRx Health. https://www.goodrx.com/well-being/diet-nutrition/are-microwaves-safe

Kass, J. (2021, February 15). *Car Maintenance 101 for teen drivers - Drive Smart Georgia*. Drive Smart Georgia. https://drivesmartgeorgia.com/blog/car-maintenance-101-teen-drivers/

KidsHealth Medical Experts. (2023, January). *How to Break Up Respectively*. TeensHealth. https://kidshealth.org/en/teens/break-up.html

Kotler, S. (2013, July 3). Learning To Learn Faster Part II: How To Read Faster And Solve Problems Like MacGyver. *Forbes*. https://www.forbes.com/sites/stevenkotler/2013/07/03/learning-to-learn-faster-part-ii/?sh=59d3f1324a00

L. Gavin, M., MD. (2022, April). *Food Portions: How Much Should I Eat?* TeensHealth. https://kidshealth.org/en/teens/portion-size.html

Laoyan, S. (2022a, October 28). Why You Should Eat the Frog First [2023] • Asana. *Asana.* https://asana.com/resources/eat-the-frog

Laoyan, S. (2022b, December 8). Learn the Pareto Principle (The 80/20 Rule) [2023] • Asana. *Asana.* https://asana.com/resources/pareto-principle-80-20-rule

Lazer, J. (2020). Novelty: The Storytelling Element Your Brain Craves. *Contently.* https://contently.com/2020/03/09/novelty-storytelling-brain-craves/#:~:text=Neuroscience%20research%20suggests%20novelty%20is,us%20to%20find%20out%20more

Lipton, B. H. (2011). *The Biology of Belief: Unleashing the Power of Consciousness, Matter & Miracles.* Hay House Incorporated.

Luenendonk, M., & Luenendonk, M. (2020, November 26). Why Your Inner Circle Should Stay Small, and How to Shrink It | Cleverism. *Cleverism.* https://www.cleverism.com/why-your-inner-circle-should-stay-small-and-how-to-shrink-it/

Maltz, M. (2015). *Psycho-Cybernetics: Updated and Expanded.* Penguin.

Marra, G. (2022, May 26). 9 interesting facts about your subconscious mind - Gail Marra Hypnotherapy. *Gail Marra Hypnotherapy.* https://www.gailmarrahypnotherapy.com/9-interesting-facts-about-your-subconscious-mind/#:~:text=Todays%20science%20estimates%20that%2095,that%20lies%20beyond%20conscious%20awareness

McManus, M. R. (2023). 12 Incredible Uses for Vinegar. *HowStuffWorks.* https://home.howstuffworks.com/green-living/vinegar-uses.htm#:~:text=Because%20this%20cheap%20pantry%20staple,water%2C%20trace%20chemicals%20and%20flavorings

Modern Teen. (n.d.). *Life Hacks - Modern Teen.* https://modernteen.co/life-hacks/

Morley, S. (2022). How to Help Your Teen Step Away from a Toxic Friendship. *Grown and Flown.* https://grownandflown.com/help-teen-step-away-from-toxic-friendship/

Muller, C., & Muller, C. (2023). How to save money as a teenager. *Money Under 30.* https://www.moneyunder30.com/how-teens-can-save-money

Murphy, P. (2021, November 14). Career Advice Tips for Teens; 13 Practical

Tips to Help You Figure it All Out. *1000 Years of Career Advice*. https://www.1000yearsofcareeradvice.com/career-advice-tips-for-teens/

Neville. (2013). *Your Faith Is Your Fortune*. Merchant Books.

Ngo, K. (2015, May 13). *55 Meaningful Quotes About Helping Others*. MotivationalWellBeing.com. https://www.motivationalwellbeing.com/55-meaningful-quotes-about-helping-others.html

Nikole. (2021, July 30). *20 Healthy Food Swaps - Healthnut Nutrition*. Healthnut Nutrition. https://www.healthnutnutrition.ca/2021/07/30/20-healthy-food-swaps/

Parent, J. (2021, May 4). *6 Car Care Tips That Teens Should Do Themselves*. Your Teen Magazine. https://yourteenmag.com/teenager-school/teens-high-school/parents-teen-driving/car-care-tips-teens

Parentingteensandtweens. (2022). 5 Ways To Prevent High School Burnout. *parentingteensandtweens.com*. https://parentingteensandtweens.com/5-ways-to-prevent-high-school-burnout/

Paulus, N. (n.d.). *Teens' Guide to Building a Strong Personal Finance Foundation*. MoneyGeek.com. https://www.moneygeek.com/financial-planning/personal-finance-for-teens/

Riebeek, H. (2009, July 7). *Planetary Motion: The History of an Idea That Launched the Scientific Revolution*. NASA Earth Observatory. https://earthobservatory.nasa.gov/features/OrbitsHistory#:~:text=In%201543%2C%20Nicolaus%20Copernicus%20detailed,century%20to%20become%20widely%20accepted

Root. (2023). 6 Convincing Benefits To Promote Reading Among Teenagers. *Nalanda International School*. https://nalandaschool.org/6-convincing-benefits-to-promote-reading-among-teenagers/

SOS Safety Magazine. (2023, February 10). Young, Dumb, & Desperate for Love: Gaining Emotional Intelligence - SOS Safety Magazine. *SOS Safety Magazine - Bullying, Abuse, Teen Suicide Issues Magazine*. https://sossafetymagazine.com/abuse/young-dumb-desperate-for-love-gaining-emotional-intelligence/

Strauss Cohen, I., Ph. D. (2017, December 26). *The Benefits of Delaying Gratification*. Psychology Today. https://www.psychologytoday.com/us/blog/your-emotional-meter/201712/the-benefits-delaying-gratification

The Jed Foundation. (2023, March 14). *How to safely end an unhealthy relation-*

ship | JED. https://jedfoundation.org/resource/how-to-safely-end-unhealthy-relationships/

The Learning Network. (2022, October 13). Teenagers Share Their Best Life Hacks. *The New York Times*. https://www.nytimes.com/2022/10/13/learning/teenagers-share-their-best-life-hacks.html

The Pomodoro Technique — Why It Works & How To Do It. (n.d.). Todoist. https://todoist.com/productivity-methods/pomodoro-technique

Thomas, J. (2022). Why human brains are not designed to multi-task. *Brain Fodder*. https://brainfodder.org/multi-tasking-doesnt-work/

UCL. (2020, April 28). *10 Benefits Of Helping Others*. Students. https://www.ucl.ac.uk/students/news/2020/apr/10-benefits-helping-others

UHBlog. (2022, March 17). How Much Water Should You Drink a Day. *University Hospitals*. https://www.uhhospitals.org/blog/articles/2022/03/how-much-water-should-you-drink-a-day

Understanding the Pareto Principle (The 80/20 Rule) – BetterExplained. (n.d.). https://betterexplained.com/articles/understanding-the-pareto-principle-the-8020-rule/

Urdaneta, I. (2022, October 6). *2022 Physics Nobel Prize Awarded to Non-Locality!* Resonance Science Foundation. https://www.resonancescience.org/blog/nobel-prize-awarded-to-non-locality#:~:text=Therefore%2C%20non%2Dlocality%20was%20proved,still%20a%20matter%20of%20debate

Wikimedia Commons contributors, "File:7 habits decision-making matrix.png," Wikimedia Commons, https://commons.wikimedia.org/w/index.php?title=File:7_habits_decision-making_matrix.png&oldid=749705624 (accessed April 12, 2023). This work is licensed under the Creative Commons Attribution-ShareAlike 4.0 International License. To view a copy of this license, visit http://creativecommons.org/licenses/by-sa/4.0/ or send a letter to Creative Commons, PO Box 1866, Mountain View, CA 94042, USA.

Wikipedia contributors. (2023). Stanford marshmallow experiment. *Wikipedia*. https://en.wikipedia.org/wiki/Stanford_marshmallow_experiment

Wong, D. (2023). The Complete List of 23 Best Memory Techniques for Studying. *Daniel Wong*. https://www.daniel-wong.com/2020/08/24/best-memory-techniques-for-students/

Woods, J. R. (2015, June 8). 11 Financial Words All Parents Should Teach Their Kids. *Forbes.* https://www.forbes.com/sites/jenniferwoods/2015/06/08/11-financial-words-all-parents-should-teach-their-kids/?sh=6ef9820c72e9

Zhang, L. (2020). The Best (and Worst) Times to Schedule an Interview. *The Muse.* https://www.themuse.com/advice/the-best-and-worst-times-to-schedule-an-interview

ABOUT THE AUTHOR

Derek T Freeman is the author of *Building Unstoppable Self-Confidence for Teens* and *88 Life-Changing High School Hacks*.

His work aims to inspire tweens, teens, parents, and families by providing motivational content and guiding them through the years that are often seen as the most challenging parts of both parenting and growing up.

As a young teenager, Derek struggled with self-esteem, bullying, and fitting in. As a father, he has attended countless groups and school functions and, along the way, has realized just how common his school experiences are. He is determined to make the turbulent waters of adolescence easier to navigate for other young people.

Derek is a musician by trade and toured the US for nine years after graduating high school, releasing six albums before the birth of his first child. He then moved into the restaurant business, managing a small team for over a decade. He has two daughters, aged 10 and 12, and a 14-year-old son.

Derek was born and raised in New York and currently lives in Connecticut with his wife, three children, and two cats.

www.ingramcontent.com/pod-product-compliance
Lightning Source LLC
Chambersburg PA
CBHW050324010526
44119CB00003B/103